APPRAISING PARTIAL
INTERESTS

Readers of this text may be interested in the following books available from the Appraisal Institute:

The Appraisal of Real Estate, eleventh edition

The Dictionary of Real Estate Appraisal, third edition

Real Estate Valuation in Litigation, second edition, by J. D. Eaton, MAI, SRA

Subdivision Analysis by Douglas D. Lovell, MAI, and Robert S. Martin, MAI, SRA

APPRAISING PARTIAL INTERESTS

By David Michael Keating, MAI

**APPRAISAL
INSTITUTE®**

875 North Michigan Avenue
Chicago, Illinois 60611

www.appraisalinstitute.org

Reviewers : Klaas Bos, SRPA, SRA
M. Rebecca Carr, MAI
Woodward S. Hanson, MAI
Jeffrey A. Johnson, MAI
Thomas A. Motta, MAI, SRA
J. Carl Schultz, Jr., MAI, SRA
John A. Schwartz, MAI

Vice President, Education: Sean Hutchinson
Director, Content Development and Quality Assurance: Margo Wright
Manager, Book Development: Stephanie Shea-Joyce
Manager, Design/Production: Julie B. Beich

For Educational Purposes Only

Nondiscrimination Policy

Library of Congress Cataloging-in-Publication Data

Keating, David Michael.
    Appraising partial interests / by David Michael Keating.
      p. cm.
    ISBN 0-922154-49-X
      1. Real property—Valuation. 2. Real property—Valuation—United States. 3.
Rental housing—Valuation. 4. Apartments—Valuation. 5. Commercial buildings—
Valuation. 6. Right of property.
    I. Title.
HD1387.K39 1998   98-16207
333.33'2—dc21   CIP

TABLE OF CONTENTS

FOREWORD

Real estate appraisers do not actually estimate the value of real estate (land and improvements), but of real property (the rights associated with owning and using real estate). Although the distinction is subtle, it is very important insofar as many appraisal assignments involve the valuation of partial interests. Because the rights to real estate can be divided in a variety of ways to serve a variety of purposes, appraisers must have a complete understanding of partial interests to perform their work competently.

Appraising Partial Interests is a practical text describing the legal, economic, and physical division of property rights to create partial interests. It provides both narrative discussion and solutions to valuation problems involving leased fee, leasehold, sandwich, and mortgage interests; life estates; conservation easements; transferable development rights; fractional interests; and subdivision and air rights. Using simple illustrations, real-world examples, and straightforward language, *Appraising Partial Interests* provides readers with an instructive and insightful examination of many complicated, but essential, value concepts.

Joseph R. Stanfield, Jr., MAI, SRA
1998 President
Appraisal Institute

ABOUT THE AUTHOR

D avid Michael Keating, MAI, is the author of the Appraisal Institute handbook, *The Valuation of Wetlands*, and presented a paper on public and private interests in real property at the Appraisal Institute National Conference in 1997. He is the author of several journal articles and served on the Young Advisory Council in 1994 and 1995. A graduate of the real estate program at the University of Florida and a fee appraiser for 11 years, Mr. Keating currently serves as a site analyst for Winn-Dixie Stores, Inc., the nation's fifth-largest grocer operating in 14 states throughout the South and mid-Atlantic states. He resides in Jacksonville, Florida, with his wife, Amy, and two children, Christopher and Carly.

INTRODUCTION

Partial interests are common and take many forms in today's dynamic marketplace. In fact, probably 95% or more of all appraisal assignments involve the valuation of "less than whole" property. Before exploring partial interest concepts, problems, and solutions, a quick overview of fundamental real property theory is helpful.

REAL ESTATE VS. REAL PROPERTY

Partial interests are a subset of real property. Specifically, real property pertains to the rights (interests) connected with real estate ownership, while real estate is the land and the improvements associated with the land. In other words, real estate is the physical *object*, while real property is the *rights* associated with owning and using the object. Often real estate is incorrectly linked with rights, a logical error insofar as real estate includes the word *estate*, which means interest or right. There are no rights associated with real estate, however; the rights pertain solely to real property.

To communicate the concept of real property, a "bundle of rights" analogy is often used. All the rights associated with real estate ownership are likened to a bundle of sticks. One stick may represent the right of quiet enjoyment, another the right of use and occupancy, another the right of transferability, and yet another the right of just compensation in the event of a public taking. The collection of all the sticks represents the sum of all real property rights in a parcel of real estate. Similarly, the sum of the value of all the sticks represents the total value of a parcel.

To use another analogy, all of the rights present in real property can be likened to an uncut pie. The whole pie can be cut into slices of various sizes and proportion, each of which represents a part of the whole (partial interest) and has value. (See Figures I.1 and I.2.)

Figure I.1 All Rights Present in Real Estate

Whole pie represents all interests.

Figure I.2 Division of Real Property Rights

Slices of pie represent various rights.

Appraisers are generally not called upon to estimate the value of the entire bundle of rights associated with real property. More often they are asked to value a particular subset, or part, of the rights present.

DIVISION OF REAL PROPERTY

The most basic division of real property is the dichotomy of private and public interests. The public interests of society are served through the governmental (public) rights of eminent domain, police power, escheat, and taxation. Private interests consist of all real property rights in a parcel of real estate exclusive of public interests. Beyond its public and private components, real property can also be divided into various economic, legal (ownership), and physical interests.

Land is one of the four agents of production necessary to generate income. The economic characteristics of real property can be divided and take on various forms, including those created by leases and mixed forms of capital. A lease subdivides the fee estate, transferring the right of use and occupancy to another in exchange for compensation in the form of rent. Partial interests created by a lease include leased fee, leasehold, and sublease interests. If a property is not financed with 100% equity, then divisions of capital are present. The most common division is into debt and equity capital through mortgage financing. Income divisions involve cash flow in the form of rent or mortgage payments.

Legal divisions of real property typically refer to the type of ownership. The two most common legal divisions are easements and life estates. In an easement, a grantee acquires the right of use and occupancy (without the payment of rent), but has no fee ownership in the particular parcel of real estate. An easement can be temporary or permanent. A construction easement associated with a road-widening project may be temporary, while a perpetual conservation easement for protection of the environment is permanent. In a life estate, a grantee enjoys the right of use and occupancy, but not ownership, of a parcel of real estate for the duration of his or her life.

There are singular and multiple forms of ownership. A sole owner enjoys 100% of the rights associated with a particular estate. For example, there is no fractional private interest (excluding public interest) involved in the sole ownership of a leased fee estate. However, when a sole ownership is divided, fractional interests are created and each owner enjoys less than 100% of the estate. The most common forms of fractional interests are tenancy by the entirety, tenancy in common, joint tenancy, and community property. Subforms include condominium, timeshare, real estate investment trust, corporate share, partnership, and cooperative interests, to name a few. Sometimes fractional interests create majority and minority positions. A majority position generally represents a controlling or managerial interest, while a minority interest does not enjoy managerial rights. General or managing partnerships, for example, typically consist of majority interests.

A direct interest is one in which active participation is called for, while an indirect interest involves passive participation, such as through a limited partnership, a share in a corporation, or another business entity. The valuation of indirect interests generally includes business valuation.

A private interest in real property can also be divided physically, usually horizontally or vertically. Horizontal division pertains to surface rights, as in subdivision and assemblage. In subdivision, parts are separated from a whole; in assemblage, parts are combined into a new whole. Vertical interests are perpendicular to horizontal interests and include various surface, subsurface, and above-surface (air) rights.

The possible variations are numerous. Figure I.3 illustrates the basic divisions and fractions of private interests in real property.

Figure I.3 Divisions and Fractions of Private Interests

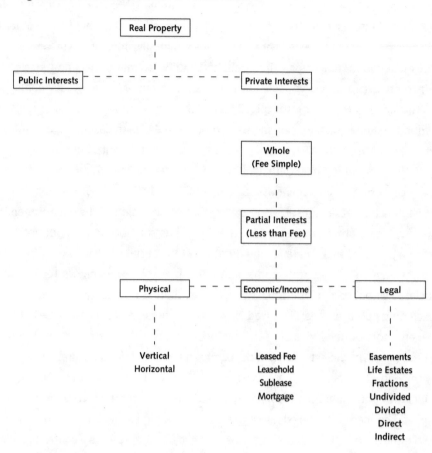

SUMMARY

Real property consists of the rights associated with real estate ownership. These rights can be divided or fractionalized into various parts. Since each right has value, each partial interest may be the subject of an appraisal. In the following chapters, the valuation of "less than whole" interests is discussed and illustrated with examples and problem solutions.

Chapters 1, 2, 3, and 4 discuss income divisions of property, including leased fee, leasehold, sandwich (sublease), and mortgage interests. Chapters 5, 6, 7, and 8 explore the legal divisions of life estates, easements, transferable development rights, and fractional interests. Chapter 9 discusses the physical division of property into horizontal and vertical interests. The epilogue puts the text material in context and considers the importance of partial interests in the future. Twenty-one valuation problems are presented in the text and illustrated with graphs and tables.

Appraising Partial Interests is a reference guide, not a sequential narrative. The text does not flow along a single river of thought. Rather, the chapters jump from one concept to another, exploring various points of interest along an educational journey. Readers should feel free to chart their own course and read the chapters in whatever order they choose. The book is brief and practical, a style which should prove useful to busy professionals looking for quick answers to complex questions.

Partial interests can appear in many forms and combinations. While problems involving partial interests vary greatly, it is hoped that the information and solutions provided here will serve as a guide to related problems encountered in the marketplace.

CHAPTER ONE

THE LEASED FEE ESTATE

A lease divides real property into income components. The most common divisions are leased fee, leasehold, and sublease (sandwich) interests. In a leased fee estate, a property owner grants another party the right to use and occupy a parcel of real estate, generally in return for compensation in the form of rent. Specifically, the leased fee estate is defined as follows:

> An ownership interest held by a landlord [lessor] with the rights of use and occupancy conveyed by lease to others [lessees]. [1] (Bracketed insertions are the author's).

The three main characteristics of the leased fee estate are: 1) the interest belongs to the lessor; 2) the rights of use and occupancy have been granted by the lessor to a separate party, the lessee; and 3) a contract known as a *lease* specifies the terms of this agreement. The transfer of rights associated with a leased fee estate are illustrated in Figure 1.1.

In a leased fee estate, the right of use and occupancy is transferred from the estate owner to a lessee in exchange for compensation in the form of rent. The amount and type of compensation has a direct bearing on the resultant value of the interest.

There are two sets of three possible scenarios which should be investigated when appraising a leased fee estate. Specifically, the two sets pertain to which party owns the improvements, if any. This must be discovered because ownership affects the amount and timing of rent payments. If the lessee owns the improvements and rents only the land,

---

1. Appraisal Institute, *The Dictionary of Real Estate Appraisal*, 3d ed. (Chicago: Appraisal Institute, 1993), 204.

Figure 1.1 Division of Rights in Leased Fee Estate

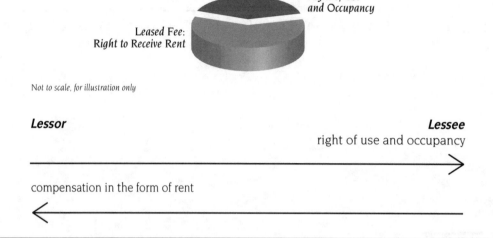

Not to scale, for illustration only

Lessor   *Lessee*

right of use and occupancy

——>

compensation in the form of rent

<——

then the lessor will not receive any income or benefits from the improvements until after the lease expires and all rights in the property revert back to the fee position. Generally, however, the lessor owns both the land and any improvements.

The three scenarios mentioned pertain to the relationship between contract rent and market rent. Contract rent is the compensation defined in the lease, while market rent is the prevailing rental rate for comparable properties in the marketplace. The scenarios are described as follows:

1. Contract rent equals market rent. In this scenario the leased fee estate is basically equivalent in value to the fee simple estate because, if the property were to become vacant, the lessor could most likely secure another tenant at approximately the same rental rate.

2. Contract rent exceeds market rent. In this scenario the value of the leased fee estate exceeds the value of the fee simple estate (depending on tenant credit risk and other factors) because, if the property were vacant, the lessor probably could not secure another tenant paying the same rental rate. Instead, a lower market rental rate would most likely be obtained. Thus, in this scenario an above-market cash flow will be received over the term of the lease, which equates to an increase in the value of the leased fee estate (and a corresponding decrease in the value of the leasehold position).

3. Contract rent is less than market rent. In this case the leased fee estate has a lower value than the fee simple estate because, if the property were vacant, the

lessor probably could secure a tenant paying at least the prevailing market rent. Therefore, a below-market cash flow is being received, which equates to a decrease in the value of the leased fee estate (and a corresponding increase in the value of the leasehold position).

EXAMPLE 1

Consider a large warehouse/distribution facility of approximately 300,000 square feet located on a 15-acre site near the airport. This Class B facility was built in the mid-1970s at dock height over a concrete slab with reinforced concrete exterior walls and a flat, built-up roof over metal decking. Although it is 25 years old, the facility has been well maintained and is structurally sound. There are 30 truck loading docks fronting a large, asphalt-paved parking area and an equal number of loading docks adjoining an active rail spur. Also present on the site is 2,000 square feet of fair-quality office space, representing less than 1% of the total building area.

Fifteen years ago the lessor, an out-of-state pension fund, leased the property to a local trucking and distribution company. The lease was for a 10-year term and included two, five-year options. The initial contract rental rate was $1.50 per square foot, triple net. The lease specifies that every five years during the term, including the option terms if exercised, the rental rate will increase by $0.20 per square foot. The tenant occupied the property for the initial 10-year term and is approaching the end of the first five-year option period. The tenant has decided to exercise the second five-year option and, beginning next month, will pay a contract rental rate of $2.10 per square foot, triple net, to lease the property.

Assume that you have been asked by the lessor (the pension fund) to appraise the market value of their leased fee estate in this parcel of real estate.

Solution

To solve an appraisal problem involving a lease, the best methodology is generally the income approach. Only in this approach can the fine details of contract rent be properly considered. The cost and sales comparison approaches are also applicable, but when above-market or below-market rents are involved, adjustments for income potential should be made.

The following data have been given:

Contract rent: $2.10 per square foot; $630,000 per year

Contract rent basis: triple net

Term of lease: 5 years

Tenant credit and payment history: Good, indicating low default risk

Market rent: $2.50 per square foot; $750,000 per year

Market rent basis: triple net

Now assume your market research reveals the following:

Current direct capitalization rate: 10.5%

Forecast terminal capitalization rate: 11.5%

Typical forecast yield rate in market: 12%

Typical market vacancy factor: 7%

Typical management fee: 1% of rent collections on triple net, long-term lease

Projected market rent inflation rate: $0.10/square foot/year

Projected market rent schedule:

Year 1:	$2.50 per square foot; $750,000 per year
Year 2:	$2.60 per square foot; $780,000 per year
Year 3:	$2.70 per square foot; $810,000 per year
Year 4:	$2.80 per square foot; $840,000 per year
Year 5:	$2.90 per square foot; $870,000 per year
Year 6:	$3.00 per square foot; $900,000 per year

Comparing forecast market rents with the contract rent schedule yields the following:

Year	Contract Rent	Market Rent	Deficit Rent
1	$630,000	$750,000	($120,000)
2	$630,000	$780,000	($150,000)
3	$630,000	$810,000	($180,000)
4	$630,000	$840,000	($210,000)
5	$630,000	$870,000	($240,000)
6	$0	$900,000	$0

Since the deficit rent is variable, a discounted cash flow analysis will be presented. In a cash flow analysis, it is important to recognize the impact on the discount rate (yield rate) resulting from a below-market rental rate.

As indicated, the typical yield rate in the market for similar properties is 12%. The applicable yield rate for this property would be lower, all else being equal, because there is less investment risk associated with a below-market rental rate than with a rate at or above market level. Specifically, if the tenant defaults, the owner of a below-market cash flow has the opportunity to re-lease the property at the higher prevailing market rent. Thus, there is only upside potential. Of course, the tenant's credit rating, the remaining term of the lease, and other such factors must also be considered. Generally, low-risk, AAA-type tenants have lower yield rates than less creditworthy tenants due to the lower risk of default. The discount rate may not vary much if the remaining term of the lease is very short.

In this example, the prevailing discount rate is 12%. It is important to note that this discount rate only applies to the favorable lease position, not to the reversion value based on a return to market rent levels. As such, a lower rate of 11% will be applied during the term of the lease and a market rate of 12% will be applied to the reversion.

To perform a cash flow analysis when a below-market rent is specified, cash flows are projected through to the point at which contract rent converts to market rent and the property achieves a stabilized position in the market. In this case a six-year cash flow analysis is presented. The analysis includes five years of contract rent and one year of rent that has returned to typical market levels. If this were a multitenant property and several of the tenants were paying below-market rents, then additional years might have been included in the analysis to consider the likelihood of increased vacancy and slower absorption of space after conversion to market rental rates .

The cash flow solution to the example is provided in Table 1.1.

Table 1.1 Cash Flow Analysis of Leased Fee Estate: Contract Rents Less Than Market Rents

Year	1	2	3	4	5	6
Contract rent	$630,000	$630,000	$630,000	$630,000	$630,000	$0
Market rent	0	0	0	0	0	900,000
Potential gross income	$630,000	$630,000	$630,000	$630,000	$630,000	$900,000
Less vacancy factor	0%	0%	0%	0%	0%	7%
Effective gross income	$630,000	$630,000	$630,000	$630,000	$630,000	$837,000
Less operating expenses:						
Management @1%	6,300	6,300	6,300	6,300	6,300	8,370
Reserves at $0.025/sq. ft.	7,500	7,500	7,500	7,500	7,500	7,500
Net operating income	$616,200	$616,200	$616,200	$616,200	$616,200	$821,130
Reversion at terminal capitalization rate of 11.5%						$7,140,261
Cash flows	$616,200	$616,200	$616,200	$616,200	$616,200	
Discount factor @11%	0.9009	0.8116	0.7312	0.6587	0.5935	
Present value of cash flows	$555,135	$500,108	$450,565	$405,891	$365,715	
Subtotal	$2,277,414					
Add present value of reversion discounted at 12%, 5 years	4,051,384					
Total	$6,328,798					
Rounded to	$6,330,000					

The value of the leased fee estate subject to the conditions and lease specifications provided is estimated to be $6,330,000

EXAMPLE 2

Consider an opposite scenario. Assume that rents are above market levels and the same market conditions presented in the previous example apply. Contract rental rates are as follows:

Year 1: $3.00 per square foot; $900,000 per year

Year 2: $3.10 per square foot; $930,000 per year

Year 3: $3.20 per square foot; $960,000 per year

Year 4: $3.30 per square foot; $990,000 per year

Year 5: $3.40 per square foot; $1,020,000 per year

Contract rent exceeds market rent as shown below.

Year	Contract Rent	Market Rent	Excess Rent
1	$900,000	$750,000	$150,000
2	$930,000	$780,000	$150,000
3	$960,000	$810,000	$150,000
4	$990,000	$840,000	$150,000
5	$1,020,000	$870,000	$150,000
6	$0	$900,000	$0

In such a scenario, the applicable discount rate would be higher due to the above-market contract rent, the potential negative effect on value in the event of tenant default, and the increased investment risk. Consequently, instead of the market-derived yield rate of 12%, a higher rate would be selected, all else being equal. In this case a discount rate of 13% is considered reasonable. Again, the reversion is discounted at the market rate since it is based on a return to market rent levels. The cash flow computations are shown in Table 1.2.

The value of the leased fee estate in this case is estimated to be $7,340,000. This is greater than the value of $6,330,000 estimated in the previous scenario. The two scenarios demonstrate that the relationship between contract and market rent has a direct impact on value. Specifically, higher rents yield higher values, all else being equal.

Table 1.2 Cash Flow Analysis of Leased Fee Estate: Contract Rent Exceeds Market Rent

Year	1	2	3	4	5	6
Contract rent	$900,000	$930,000	$960,000	$990,000	$1,020,000	$0
Market rent	0	0	0	0	0	900,000
Potential gross income	$900,000	$930,000	$960,000	$990,000	$1,020,000	$900,000
Less vacancy factor	0%	0%	0%	0%	0%	7%
Effective gross income	$900,000	$930,000	$960,000	$990,000	$1,020,000	$837,000
Less operating expenses:						
Management @1%	9,000	9,300	9,600	9,900	10,200	8,370
Reserves at $0.025/sq ft	7,500	7,500	7,500	7,500	7,500	7,500
Net operating income	$883,500	$913,200	$942,900	$972,600	$1,002,300	$821,130
Reversion at terminal capitalization rate of 11.5%						$7,140,261
Cash flows	$883,500	$913,200	$942,900	$972,600	$1,002,300	
Discount factor @13%	0.8850	0.7831	0.6931	0.6133	0.5428	
Present value of cash flows	$781,898	$715,127	$653,524	$596,496	$544,048	
Subtotal	$3,291,093					
Add present value of reversion discounted at 12%, 5 years	4,051,384					
Total	$7,342,477					
Rounded to	$7,340,000					

EXAMPLE 3

There is another way to solve leased fee valuation problems, especially when level income is projected. This alternative method involves direct capitalization. The appraiser estimates the fee simple value of the property based on market rent levels and conditions and then adds the present value of the excess rent (or deficit rent) as applicable. An alternative method for solving Example 2, the scenario specifying above-market rents, begins with an estimate of value based on market rents, market vacancy, market capitalization rates, and other market parameters as set forth below.

Potential gross income based on market rents	$750,000
Less 7% allowance for vacancy and collection loss	52,500
Effective gross income	$697,500

Less operating expenses:	
Management @ 1%	6,975
Reserves @ $0.025/sq. ft.	7,500
Net operating income	$683,025
Capitalized @ 10.5%	$6,505,000

To this value the appraiser adds the value contribution of the excess rent resulting from the favorable lease. As previously shown, this excess rent equates to a forecast level payment of $150,000 per year for five years. Since this excess rent is forecast to remain level over the five-year lease term, direct capitalization can be applied.

Implicit in direct capitalization is both a return *of* and a return *on* investment. The excess rent in this case is for five years and includes no reversionary value. After the lease expires, the contract rent will probably be reduced to market levels, thus eliminating any reversion associated with the above-market rent payments. Therefore, all investment in the excess rent cash flow must be returned over the lease period. The return of investment, also known as the *rate of recapture*, can be estimated using either a straight-line or sinking fund method. Applying a sinking fund method at the market yield rate of 12% yields a return of investment of 0.1574, or approximately 15.75% per year.

A return on investment must be considered to reflect the cost of capital. Assume that market research reveals the rate is 10%. Considering these data, the direct capitalization rate associated with the excess rent is estimated as follows:

	Return of investment	15.75%
+	Return on investment	10.00%
=	Capitalization rate	25.75%

Capitalizing the annual excess rent of $150,000 yields the following:

	Excess rent	$150,000
÷	Cap rate	25.75%
=	Value	$582,524

This value is then added to the market rent value previously calculated to indicate the total value of the leased fee estate.

	Fee simple value	$6,505,000
+	Value of excess rent	$582,524
=	Total leased fee value	$7,087,524
	Rounded to	$7,090,000

Note that direct capitalization yields a slightly lower estimate of value than discounted cash flow (DCF) analysis. Direct capitalization resulted in a value of $7,090,000, while the DCF analysis produced a value of $7,340,000—a variance of 3.5% even though the inputs were the same. One reason for this variance is that direct capitalization uses current market rent levels of $750,000, while DCF analysis uses projected market rent levels. When the amount of excess (or deficit) rent is level, direct capitalization is the easiest and least speculative method to apply. When the amount is not level, but variable, a discounted cash flow analysis may be necessary. The key to applying DCF analysis is accurately forecasting income streams and recognizing the appropriate discount rate.

SUMMARY

The leased fee estate is a form of divided interest established by a lease. A lease is a contractual agreement between a property owner and a tenant in which the owner (lessor) generally grants the tenant (lessee) the right to use and occupy a property for a period of time in exchange for compensation in the form of contract rent. The value of the resulting leased fee estate can be estimated based on a careful analysis of the lease and contract rent agreement.

There are two sets of three possible scenarios resulting from a lease. The two sets pertain to which party owns the land and improvements, if any. The three scenarios are: 1) contract rent equals market rent, 2) contract rent exceeds market rent, and 3) contract rent is less than market rent.

The best methodology to apply when appraising the leased fee estate is the income approach because it allows the appraiser to perform a careful analysis of the rent compensation associated with the owner's interest. The cost and sales comparison approaches can also be applied, but if contract rent differs from market rent, adjustments for income potential are warranted. As demonstrated, both direct capitalization and discounted cash flow analysis may be applied.

CHAPTER TWO

THE LEASEHOLD ESTATE

T he leasehold estate is the interest created by a lease that is held by the tenant (lessee). The owner of this interest has the right to use and occupy a parcel of real estate for a specified period of time in exchange for compensation to the landlord (lessor), generally in the form of contract rent. The leasehold estate is defined as follows:

> The interest held by the lessee through a lease conveying the rights of use and occupancy for a stated term under certain conditions.[1]

The three primary characteristics of a leasehold estate are: 1) the interest belongs to the lessee, 2) the interest has been granted by a lessor and includes the right of use and occupancy for a stated period of time, and 3) a contract known as a *lease* specifies the terms of this agreement.

The appraisal of a leasehold estate (like the appraisal of a leased fee as discussed in Chapter 1), requires consideration of two sets of three possible scenarios. Again, these sets are a function of which party owns the improvements to the land. A tenant may rent both land and improvements to the land, such as a warehouse that is completely owned by the landlord, or the tenant may rent only the land from the landlord and develop and own the improvements to the land. In the latter case, the tenant owns the improvements

---

1. Appraisal Institute, *The Dictionary of Real Estate Appraisal,* 3d ed. (Chicago: Appraisal Institute, 1993), 204.

for the duration of the lease, but ownership will revert to the landlord at the termination of the lease agreement. This situation is not common and is typically found only in conjunction with very long-term lease arrangements.

The three scenarios which may be applicable in a leasehold valuation are similar to those discussed in regard to the leased fee in Chapter 1.

1. Contract rent equals market rent. In this scenario the leasehold interest basically has no value unless the improvements are owned by the tenant. Because the rent being paid by the tenant represents the rent that the tenant would most likely pay at any comparable facility, no positive or negative position is established. However, the potential for value could exist depending on the duration of the lease term.

2. Contract rent is lower than market rent. In this scenario the leasehold interest could have positive value beyond the value of any improvements that may be owned by the tenant. The value is positive if the lease agreement permits subletting and a significant lease period remains. In this case the tenant could potentially sublease the property and enjoy the positive cash flow differential between contract rent and market rent. Even if the lease does not allow subletting, it may be valuable to the tenant for its use value and opportunity cost savings over market rent levels. If the lease agreement can be canceled or has a very short remaining term, however, it is unlikely that the leasehold position is marketable or has much value.

3. Contract rent exceeds market rent. In this case the leasehold estate has negative value, not considering any potential positive value resulting from tenant-owned improvements, if applicable. The value is negative because the tenant is paying more than the typical market rent. As a result, the value of the leased fee increases.

The relationship between the rights and compensation exchanged over the term of a lease is illustrated in Figure 2.1.

Figure 2.1 looks like Figure 1.1 in the previous chapter because the leasehold estate is the opposite component of the leased fee estate, the other interest created by a lease agreement. The relationship between lessor and lessee is the same, but the interest being valued in the following examples is the one associated with the lessee.

EXAMPLE 4

Assume the same scenario relating to the 300,000-sq.-ft. warehouse/distribution property discussed in the preceding chapter. The tenant is paying a contract rental rate of $2.10 per

Figure 2.1 Division of Rights in Leasehold Estate

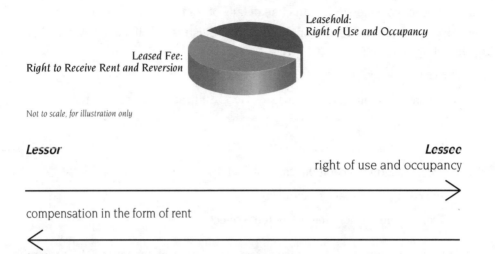

Leasehold:
Right of Use and Occupancy

Leased Fee:
Right to Receive Rent and Reversion

Not to scale, for illustration only

Lessor   **Lessee**

right of use and occupancy

———————————————————————————————————————→

compensation in the form of rent

←———————————————————————————————————————

square foot, triple net, for the property, and this rent will remain constant for the remaining five-year term of the lease. Research reveals that market rental rates are $2.50 per square foot, triple net, and are forecast to increase at $0.05 per square foot per year over the next five years as shown below:

Year	Market Rent/Sq. Ft.
1	$2.50
2	$2.55
3	$2.60
4	$2.65
5	$2.70

Obviously, market rents are expected to exceed contract rents for the duration of the lease term. The differences are set forth as follows:

Year	Market Rent/Sq.Ft.	Contract Rent/Sq.Ft.	Difference Per Sq.Ft.	Dollar Difference
1	$2.50	$2.10	$0.40	$120,000
2	$2.55	$2.10	$0.45	$135,000
3	$2.60	$2.10	$0.50	$150,000
4	$2.65	$2.10	$0.55	$165,000
5	$2.70	$2.10	$0.60	$180,000

Solution

As in the leased fee valuation, the best methodology to apply is the income approach, which allows for consideration of the fine details of contract rent. The cost and sales comparison approaches are also applicable, but adjustments will be necessary when above- or below-market rents are involved.

The following additional information is given:

Tenant credit and payment history: Good, indicating low default risk

Typical market yield rate: 12%

Current direct capitalization rate: 10.5%

Forecast terminal capitalization rate: 11.5%

Typical market vacancy factor: 7%

Typical management fee: 1% of rent collections

Assume for this example that the lease agreement allows the tenant to sublet the property without any penalty or restrictions as long as the lessee remains liable for all contract rent payments and lease stipulations.

The cash flow analysis to value the leasehold estate should project income through to the termination of the lease. After this point, the lessee will no longer have any rights in the property and future cash flows are not relevant. Thus, a five-year cash flow analysis is performed to correspond to the remaining five-year lease term. Some other factors to consider are described below.

- The cash flow to the leasehold estate is the difference between contract and market rents. In this case, contract rent is below market rent and the leasehold position enjoys a positive potential cash flow.

- To estimate the effective cash flow, a vacancy factor must be deducted (to correspond with the market rental rates). The market vacancy factor in this example is 7%. However, if the lessee has already secured a creditworthy subtenant of good quality for the term of the original lease, no vacancy factor would apply.

- A management expense should also be deducted. A sublease situation would require management by the lessee. In this example, the management expense is 1% of effective rental income.

- No reserves for replacement or capital expenditure allowance is required unless the leasehold position owns the improvements and the remaining term of the lease is long.

- The discount rate is a function of the leasehold position and the status of cash flows, i.e., whether the cash flow is above or below market levels. In general, the discount rate associated with a leasehold interest is higher than that associated with a leased fee interest because a leasehold has no reversionary benefits, and thus no potential appreciation. Assume in this example that the applicable discount rate is 13%. A full cash flow solution is provided in Table 2.1.

Table 2.1 Cash Flow Analysis of Leasehold Estate: Contract Rent Less Than Market Rent

Year	1	2	3	4	5	6
Market rental rate/sq. ft.	$2.50	$2.55	$2.60	$2.65	$2.70	$2.75
Potential market rental income	$750,000	$765,000	$780,000	$795,000	$810,000	$825,000
Contract rental rate/sq. ft.	$2.10	$2.10	$2.10	$2.10	$2.10	$0
Contract rental income	$630,000	$630,000	$630,000	$630,000	$630,000	$0
Potential gross income	$120,000	$135,000	$150,000	$165,000	$180,000	$0
Less vacancy factor	7%	7%	7%	7%	7%	7%
Effective gross income	$111,600	$125,550	$139,500	$153,450	$167,400	$0
Less operating expenses:						
Management @1%	$1,116	$1,256	$1,395	$1,534	$1,674	$0
Net operating income	$110,484	$124,294	$138,105	$151,916	$165,726	$0
Reversion at terminal capitalization rate of 11.5%					$0	
Cash flows	$110,484	$124,294	$138,105	$151,916	$165,726	
Discount factor @13%	0.8850	0.7831	0.6931	0.6133	0.5428	
Present value of cash flows	$97,778	$97,335	$95,721	$93,170	$89,956	
Total present value	$473,960					
Rounded to	$475,000					

The value of the leasehold estate subject to the conditions and lease specifications provided is estimated to be $475,000. If the contract rent were above market levels, the value of the leasehold position would be negative, indicating an increase in the value of the leased fee estate.

EXAMPLE 5

In Example 4 the lessor was assumed to own both the land and improvements, which is typical in most lease agreements. What happens when the lessee owns the improvements? This example examines such a case.

Consider the same general property characteristics discussed in the preceding examples— i.e., 15 acres of land improved with a 300,000-sq.-ft., Class B warehouse/ distribution facility. Now assume that the lessor owns only the 15 acres of land, while the lessee owns the improvements and enjoys the right to use and occupy the underlying land for a remaining lease term of 40 years. The lease agreement specifies the following:

> Lease origination date: 10 years ago
>
> Date improvements were constructed: 10 years ago
>
> Original term of lease: 50 years
>
> Remaining term of lease: 40 years
>
> Current land lease rate: $0.05 per square foot per year; $32,670
>
> Lease basis: triple net
>
> Current land capitalization rate in market: 10%
>
> Current land value based on comparable sales: $0.50 per square foot; $22,000 per acre.
>
> Forecast land yield rate: 11%

Solutions

Valuing a leasehold estate in which the lessee owns the improvements is not as simple as estimating value when the lessor owns both the land and improvements. The remaining term of the lease dictates which approach is applied. In this example, the remaining term of the lease is long—40 years—so all three approaches can be applied.

Cost approach application. In the cost approach the replacement or reproduction cost new of the improvements is estimated and a deduction is made for depreciation. The rate of depreciation, also known as the *rate of recapture*, is a function of the age and condition of the improvements as well as the remaining term of the lease.

In this case assume that research reveals the replacement cost of the warehouse is $16.50 per square foot, and the typical economic life of similar improvements is 50 years. The subject improvements are 10 years old, indicating a remaining life of 40 years, which corresponds to the remaining term of the lease. Applying a straight-line rate of recapture yields the following estimate of depreciation via the age-life method:

10 years / 50 years = 20%

The cost approach computations follow:

Replacement cost of building:	
$16.50/sq. ft. (inclusive) x 300,000 sq. ft.	$4,950,000
Replacement cost of site improvements:	
Paving, fencing, etc.	$200,000
Total replacement cost	$5,150,000

Less depreciation at 20% (age-life method)	1,030,000
Depreciated cost	$4,120,000
Per square foot	
$4,120,000 / 300,000 sq. ft.	$13.73

No land value is added because the leasehold estate does not own the land. However, depending on the land lease rate, the lessee may also have an interest in the underlying land. In this example land values were given at $0.50 per square foot, with land capitalization rates of 10%. Therefore, the market rent due the land is calculated as follows:

$$I_L = V_L \times R_L$$

where:
I_L = Income to the land
V_L = Land value
R_L = Land capitalization rate

Substituting numbers into the formula yields:

$$I_L = \$0.50 \text{ per square foot} \times 10\%$$
$$= \$0.05 \text{ per square foot}$$

The income to the land reflects a rental rate equal to the current contract rental rate, so there is no leasehold value in the land. If the contract rent had been lower than market rent, leasehold value in the land would be present and would be added to the cost approach computations.

Sales comparison approach application. The sales comparison approach may be applied when the lessee owns the improvements. The land extraction method of the sales comparison approach allows for direct comparison of the subject and comparable improvements. The key to applying this approach properly is to identify comparable sales that share not only similar physical characteristics, but also have similar ages and remaining economic lives.

The 300,000-sq.-ft., Class B warehouse/distribution facility being appraised is reported to have an age of 10 years and a remaining lease term of 40 years. Market research reveals the economic life of similar improvements generally ranges from 45 to 55 years. Thus the land value components of these comparable sales can be estimated and extracted from their sale prices to yield the value contribution of the improvements. The resultant improvement values can then be compared to the subject improvements and used as indicators of value.

Assume the appraiser finds a recent sale of a 325,000-sq.-ft., Class B warehouse/ distribution facility on a 10-acre site in the subject neighborhood. The facility is nine years old, has rail service, and is similar in functional utility and condition to the subject. It was sold for $4,500,000. Comparable vacant industrial sites in the area have been selling for $0.50 per square foot, on average, indicating that the land value associated with this comparable sale is $217,800 (10 acres x 43,560 square feet per acre x $0.50 per square foot). The value contribution of the improvements is extracted as follows:

$$\begin{array}{rl} & \text{Total sale price} \\ - & \text{Value of underlying land} \\ \hline = & \text{Value of improvements} \end{array}$$

Substituting numbers into the formula produces the following results:

$$\begin{array}{rl} & \$4,500,000 \\ - & 217,800 \\ \hline = & \$4,282,200 \end{array}$$

Dividing this indicated improvement value by the size of the improvements yields a unit value of $13.18 per square foot ($4,282,200/ 325,000) for the comparable. This unit value can then be compared to the subject and applied as an indicator of value. The same procedure should be applied to several comparable sales to derive a well-supported estimate of value. If the sales analyzed indicate unit values ranging from $12.00 to $14.00 per square foot, the following value estimate would be reasonable:

300,000 sq. ft. x $13.00/sq. ft. = $3,900,000

Income approach application. The income approach is probably the best indicator of value for properties with above- or below-market rents. In this approach the value of the leasehold estate is estimated as the income-earning potential of the property minus the land lease payment over the term of the lease. Assume the following additional information has been given:

Market rent for property (land and improvements): $2.50 per square foot; $750,000

Typical market basis: triple net

Typical market vacancy rate: 7%

Typical market management fee: 1%

Forecast property yield rate: 12%

Current capitalization rate: 10.5%

Considering these inputs, the following net income calculations can be made:

Potential gross income (as if unencumbered):

300,000 sq. ft. x $2.50/sq. ft.	$750,000
Less 7% allowance for vacancy loss	52,500
Effective gross income	$697,500
Less operating expenses:	
Management @ 1%	$6,975
Reserves for replacement @ $0.025/sq. ft.	7,500
Subtotal	$683,025
Less land lease rent payment	
(15 ac. x 43,560 sq. ft./ac. x $0.05/sq. ft.)	32,670
Net operating income to leasehold interest	$650,355

In estimating an appropriate capitalization rate, both the return of investment (recapture) and the return on investment must be considered. The return of investment is a function of the remaining term of the lease. As previously stated, the remaining term is 40 years, so the straight-line rate of recapture would be 2.5%, calculated as follows:

$$1 \text{ year} / 40 \text{ years} = 0.025$$

Instead of a straight-line rate of recapture, an appraiser could apply a sinking fund factor rate at the anticipated investor yield rate. The appropriate rate and method of application should be based on market research in an attempt to mirror the expectations of investors in the market.

The return of investment would be higher than the overall property capitalization rate, reported to be 10.5%, because the overall property rate (R_o) includes a land component, which would not apply in estimating a building capitalization rate. Land yield rates are generally lower than improvement yield rates because the land carries lower risk and there is no need for recapture. Moreover, the rate associated with a leasehold position is higher than the rate associated with a leased fee position because the leasehold does not enjoy reversionary benefits. For this example, assume a return on investment of 13.5%.

The building capitalization rate is estimated as follows:

	Return on
+	Return of
=	Cap rate

Or,

	13.5%
+	2.5%
=	16.0%

Capitalizing the net income to the improvements by the improvement capitalization rate yields the following leasehold value:

$$\$650,355 / 0.16 = \$4,064,719$$

Rounded to $4,065,000, or $13.55 per square foot of building area

The value estimates resulting from the three approaches applied in this example are summarized as follows:

Cost approach	$4,120,000
Sales comparison approach	$3,900,000
Income approach	$4,065,000

All three approaches yield fairly consistent value indications and a reconciled value estimate of $4,000,000 appears reasonable.

SUMMARY

The leasehold estate is established through a lease, a contractual agreement between a property owner and a tenant. This estate is held by the tenant and its value can be estimated based on a careful analysis of the lease agreement. When appraising a leasehold estate, two sets of three possible scenarios may be considered depending on which party owns the improvements to the land.

Specifically, a tenant may rent land and the improvements to the land or a tenant may rent only the land and own the improvements. In the latter case, the tenant owns the improvements for the duration of the lease, but ownership reverts to the landlord at the termination of the lease agreement. More commonly, tenants rent both land and improvements.

The three leasehold scenarios are: 1) contract rent equals market rent, 2) contract rent is lower than market rent, and 3) contract rent exceeds market rent. The best methodology to apply when appraising a leasehold estate is the income approach because it includes a careful analysis of these possible rent scenarios. The cost and sales comparison approaches can also be applied, but generally only when the term of the lease is fairly long or when the tenant owns the improvements.

CHAPTER THREE

THE SANDWICH LEASE POSITION

he sandwich lease position is a form of leasehold estate created by a sublease. Such an estate may exist only if the lease agreement allows the tenant the privilege of subletting. This position is defined as follows:

> An agreement in which the lessee in a prior lease conveys to
> a third party the same interest that the lessee enjoys (the
> right of use and occupancy of the property), but for a shorter
> [or equal] term than that of the lessee.[1] (Bracketed insertion
> is the author's.)

In effect, there are two tenants in a sandwich position: the original tenant and a subtenant. The owner of the sandwich interest is the original tenant, who transfers the right to use and occupy a parcel of real estate to another tenant for a specified period of time in exchange for compensation, generally in the form of contract rent. Figure 3.1 illustrates the relationships associated with a sandwich arrangement.

As discussed in regard to the leased fee and leasehold estates in Chapters 1 and 2, three possible scenarios may be considered in appraising a sandwich lease position. All involve the relationship between contract rent and market rent. These scenarios are described as follows:

---

1. Appraisal Institute, *The Appraisal of Real Estate,* 11th ed. (Chicago: Appraisal Institute, 1996), 142.

1. The contract rental rate of the subtenant is equal to the contract rental rate of the original tenant. In this scenario the sandwich position does not have any measurable value because it is not realizing a positive or negative cash flow. Instead, the rent it receives is passed through to the original lessor. This is actually a liability to the original tenant, who incurs management expenses and the risk of subtenant default.

2. The contract rental rate of the subtenant exceeds the contract rental rate of the original tenant. In this scenario the sandwich position enjoys a positive cash flow and, thus, a generally positive value. The value of this position is a function of the amount of cash flow, the subtenant's credit rating, the remaining term of the lease, and other factors.

3. The contract rental rate of the subtenant is less than the contract rental rate of the original tenant. In this scenario the sandwich position experiences a negative cash flow because its liabilities exceed its value.

Figure 3.1 Relationships in a Sandwich Lease

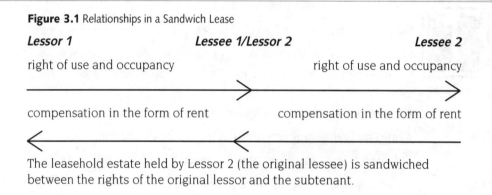

The leasehold estate held by Lessor 2 (the original lessee) is sandwiched between the rights of the original lessor and the subtenant.

EXAMPLE 6

Assume the 300,000-sq.-ft. warehouse/distribution facility discussed in the previous chapters is again the subject of an appraisal assignment. In this case, however, Tenant 1, the original lessee, recently vacated the facility and moved into a larger warehouse nearby. Subsequently, the old facility was subleased to another lessee, Tenant 2. The appraiser has been asked by the original tenant (Tenant 1) to appraise the market value of the company's interest in this parcel of real estate.

Tenant 1 is paying a contract rental rate of $2.00 per square foot, triple net, for 10 years. Tenant 2 is paying a contract rental rate of $2.25 per square foot, also triple net for 10 years. Thus, the contract rent of the subtenant exceeds the contract rent of the original tenant by $0.25 per square foot for the remaining term of the original lease.

Solution

To solve an appraisal problem involving a sandwich lease, the best methodology is the income approach. As indicated previously, only in this approach can the fine details of contract rent be properly considered. The following additional data are given:

> Tenant 1's contract rent: $2.00 per square foot; $600,000 per year
>
> Contract rent basis: triple net
>
> Remaining term of lease: 10 years
>
> Tenant 2's contract rent: $2.25 per square foot; $675,000 per year
>
> Market rent basis: triple net
>
> Term of subtenant lease: 10 years
>
> Current direct capitalization rate: 10.5%
>
> Typical forecast yield rate in market: 12%
>
> Typical management fee: 5% of rent collections

The value of a sandwich position is generally equal to the present value of the cash flow difference between the rent received and the rent paid. Both direct capitalization and discounted cash flow (DCF) analysis can be applied to solve this type of problem. In this example, a DCF analysis is discussed. In the following example, direct capitalization will be applied.

In the DCF analysis of this problem, the applicable discount rate (yield rate) is a function of the subtenant's credit rating and the level of contract rent as compared to market rent. In general, there is more risk associated with a sandwich lease position than a typical leased fee position due to the lack of reversionary benefits. Moreover, the subleasehold position has more risk than the original leasehold due to its subservient orientation. Thus, assume the discount rate applicable in this case is 14%.

In a cash flow analysis of a sandwich lease position, cash flows are projected through to the end of the subtenant's lease. After that, there is no sandwich position. A 10-year cash flow analysis of the sandwich lease position is presented in Table 3.1.

Table 3.1 Cash Flow Analysis of Sandwich Lease Position

Year	1	2	3	4	5	6	7	8	9	10
Subtenant's contract rent	$675,000	$675,000	$675,000	$675,000	$675,000	$675,000	$675,000	$675,000	$675,000	$675,000
Less:										
Management expense @ 1%	6,750	6,750	6,750	6,750	6,750	6,750	6,750	6,750	6,750	6,750
Original contract rent	600,000	600,000	600,000	600,000	600,000	600,000	600,000	600,000	600,000	600,000
Net income to sandwich position	$68,250	$68,250	$68,250	$68,250	$68,250	$68,250	$68,250	$68,250	$68,250	$68,250
Present value factor at discount rate of 14%	0.8772	0.7695	0.6750	0.5921	0.5194	0.4556	0.3996	0.3506	0.3075	0.2697
Present value of cash flows	$59,869	$52,518	$46,069	$40,411	$35,449	$31,095	$27,273	$23,928	$20,987	$18,407
Total present value	$356,006									
Rounded to	$356,000									

The value of the sandwich lease position in this example is estimated to be $356,000.

EXAMPLE 7

The direct capitalization approach can also be applied. As shown, the sandwich position enjoys a positive net income of $68,250 per year for 10 years. There is no reversion, so all of the investment must be recaptured over the term of the lease. The straight-line rate of recapture (return of investment) would be 10%, calculated as one year divided by the 10-year lease term. Alternatively, a sinking fund factor at the market yield rate could be applied as it was in Example 5 in Chapter 1.

To the rate of recapture the appraiser must add a return *on* the investment (the cash-on-cash rate of return). Assume that market research reveals this rate to be 10%. The direct capitalization rate is calculated as follows:

$$\begin{array}{rl} & \text{Return on investment} \\ + & \text{Return of investment} \\ \hline & \text{Capitalization rate} \end{array}$$

Or

$$\begin{array}{rl} & 10\% \\ + & 10\% \\ \hline & 20\% \end{array}$$

Note that this rate is well above the overall property capitalization rate of 10.5%, and it should be higher due to the greater risk of the position (behind the leased fee), the lack of reversionary benefits, and other factors. It is also lower than the 25.75% rate applied in Example 3 because the term of recapture in this example is 10 years, as compared to five years in that example. As can be seen, many factors can influence the appropriate capitalization rate.

Capitalizing the net income of $68,250 per year at 20% yields a resultant sandwich lease value of $341,000. This indication is very similar to the value of $356,000 resulting from the discounted cash flow analysis.

SUMMARY

The sandwich lease position is a form of leasehold estate. In a sandwich arrangement, the original lessee becomes a lessor as a result of a sublease arrangement. Such a position may exist if the lease agreement allows for subletting. The value of this position is estimated through careful analysis of lease and contract rent terms.

When appraising a sandwich lease, two sets of three possible scenarios may be present. The two sets are a function of which party owns the improvements to the land. Generally a tenant will rent both land and improvements to the land. Sometimes, however, the tenant rents the land but owns the improvements. Who owns the land and improvements has a direct impact on the market rental payment due the position.

The three possible sandwich lease scenarios are: 1) the contract rental rate of the subtenant may be equal to the contract rental rate of the original tenant; 2) the contract rental rate of the subtenant may exceed the contract rental rate of the original tenant, in which case the sandwich position enjoys positive cash flow and positive value; and 3) the contract rental rate of the subtenant may be less than the contract rental rate of the original tenant, in which case the sandwich position experiences negative cash flow and its liabilities exceed its value.

The best methodology to apply when appraising a sandwich lease position is the income approach. Both direct capitalization and DCF analysis are applicable if they include a careful analysis of the possible rent scenarios and risks present. Generally there are insufficient sales to apply the sales comparison approach and the cost approach only applies if the sandwich position owns the improvements. Even then, special considerations must be made for the remaining term of the lease.

CHAPTER FOUR

MORTGAGE INTERESTS

 wo forms of capital are used to finance real property—debt and equity. The most common form of real estate debt is a mortgage, an economic division of real property defined as:

> A pledge of a described property interest as collateral or security
> for the repayment of a loan under certain terms and conditions. [1]

A mortgage is created when a mortgagor, or borrower, pledges real property as collateral for repayment of a loan. The mortgagee is the lender who accepts the mortgage as collateral. Mortgages involve pledged real estate and thus are linked to real property.

The cost of borrowing debt capital is reflected in the interest rate associated with repayment of the mortgage. In case of investment failure, borrower default, or foreclosure, the debt position has priority over the equity position. Thus, lenders get paid back first, and the debt position typically involves less risk than the equity position and yields a correspondingly lower cost of capital (interest rate).

There are several types of mortgages: first, second, and third mortgages; guaranteed, insured, and conventional mortgages; institutional and private mortgages; and fixed-rate and variable-rate mortgages, among others. Mortgages identified as first, second, third, etc., refer to the status of the lien position. A first mortgage has priority lien over all other mortgages, a second mortgage is subordinated to the first mortgage but has priority over a third mortgage, and so on. This priority of lien has a direct impact on the level of risk

1. Appraisal Institute, *The Dictionary of Real Estate Appraisal,* 3d ed. (Chicago: Appraisal Institute, 1993), 233.

associated with repayment of the mortgage. If there are no proceeds left after the first position is satisfied, the remaining mortgagees have no means of collateral repayment. As a result, the interest rate on a mortgage typically increases as its position is subordinated.

Guaranteed, insured, and conventional mortgages refer to the status of repayment risk. In a guaranteed mortgage, repayment is guaranteed. The Veterans Administration (VA) is the most common guarantor of mortgages and provides this service to current and former members of the armed forces. With an insured mortgage, repayment is insured. The Federal Housing Administration (FHA) is commonly involved with insured loans and assesses borrowers a fee to pay for this insurance. Loans insured by the FHA are subject to restrictions regarding maximum loan amounts, qualifying ratios, types of homes funded, etc. A conventional loan does not include any guarantees or insurance and has fewer restrictions and limitations. However, when conventional mortgages are used, lenders typically require borrowers to insure repayment of the loan by purchasing private mortgage insurance (PMI) if the loan-to-value ratio is greater than 80%. Guarantees and insurance reduce lender risk and thus serve to lower interest rates and free the flow of debt capital.

The terms *institutional mortgage* and *private mortgage* refer to the status of the lender. Institutional lenders include the government, banks, credit unions, pension funds, and insurance companies. A private mortgage involves an individual or noninstitutional lender. The most common form of private mortgage is seller financing, in which the seller of a property holds the mortgage pledged by the buyer. There are some unique advantages to private mortgages. Private mortgages generally offer the borrower lower costs and looser underwriting requirements. The lender, or seller, can defer capital gains taxes and may attract a buyer for a less marketable parcel of real estate via favorable financing arrangements.

Fixed-rate mortgages have a fixed rate of interest over the life of the loan, thus creating a level repayment stream. In contrast, variable-rate mortgages (also known as *adjustable rate mortgages*, or ARMs) call for a floating interest rate, resulting in a fluctuating repayment stream. Variable-rate mortgages typically are linked to an index, such as the prime lending rate or the yield rates on treasury bonds, with a fixed spread. For example, the interest rate may be linked to movement in the 10-year treasury bond rate and the spread may be fixed at 1%. If the yield on a 10-year treasury bond increases from 6% to 7%, then the mortgage interest rate would increase from 7% to 8%. Rate adjustments are typically limited to one per year and most mortgages specify a lifetime limit, or cap.

EXAMPLE 8

Assume a parcel of real estate has been acquired for $200,000 and the acquisition was financed with $50,000 cash (25% equity) and a $150,000 mortgage (75% debt). The mortgage calls for a 30-year note amortized (repaid) monthly at an interest rate of 10%. What is the value of the mortgage interest in the property after five years of payments (25 years remaining on the note) if market interest rates on similar mortgages decrease to 8.5%?

The division of capital and transfer of interests involved with this example are illustrated in Figure 4.1.

Figure 4.1 Division of Capital into Debt and Equity Interests

Debt   *Equity*

Not to scale, for illustration only

Mortgagor   ***Mortgagee***

Repayment of borrowed capital at interest rate

⟶

Use of borrowed capital

⟵

There are two steps involved in estimating the value of a fixed-rate mortgage in response to changing interest rates. The payment associated with the mortgage note is calculated and then discounted at the current yield rate. To calculate the monthly payment, the following formula can be applied:

Payment = loan amount x payment factor

where:

Payment factor $= I / (1 - \text{present value factor})$

I = interest rate

Present value factor $= 1 / (1 + I)^n$

Inserting the figures given in the example (10% interest rate and monthly payments), the payment factor can be calculated as follows:

Factor $= (0.10/12) / (1 - (1 / (1 + 0.10/12)^{30 \times 12})$

$= (0.00833) / (1 - (1 / (1 + 0.00833)^{360})$

$$= (0.00833) / (1 - (1 / 19.81381))$$
$$= (0.00833) / (1 - 0.05047)$$
$$= (0.00833) / (0.94953)$$
$$= 0.00877$$

Applying this factor to the loan amount generates the following monthly payment:

$$\text{Payment} \quad = \$150{,}000 \times 0.00877$$
$$= \$1{,}316$$

The next step in the analysis is to discount the payment over the remaining term of the mortgage at the current yield rate. In this example, yield rates on mortgages are reported to be 8.5%, down from 10% when the note was originated. Therefore, the applicable discount rate is 8.5%, and the remaining term is 300 months (25 years x 12 months/year). The present value factor of a payment for 300 periods (25 years) at 0.708% per period (8.5% divided by 12 months) is 124.247, calculated as follows:

$$\text{Annuity factor} \quad = (1 - (1 / (1 + I^n))) / I$$
$$= (1 - (1 / (1 + 0.085/12)^{300})) / 0.085/12$$
$$= (1 - (1 / (1.00708)^{300})) / 0.00708$$
$$= (1 - (1 / 8.31041)) / 0.00708$$
$$= (1 - 0.12033) / 0.00708$$
$$= 0.87967 / 0.00708$$
$$= 124.247$$

Applying this annuity factor to the payment of $1,316 per month indicates the value of the mortgage is $163,509.

In this example, the value of the mortgage exceeds the original loan amount of $150,000, even though five years of payments have been made on the note. This is because market interest rates have fallen below the original interest rate, making the note more valuable. Note, the drop is only 150 basis points, from 10% to 8.5%, so the mortgagee may not yet be willing to incur the costs of refinancing to secure a lower interest rate loan and the loan may be marketable at less discount. In contrast, if market interest rates had risen, the value of the note would have fallen.

For instance, consider the same parameters but assume that market interest rates on comparable mortgages have increased to 12%. The annuity factor in this case would decrease to 94.94655, which, when applied to the payment of $1,316 per month, yields a resultant mortgage value of $124,950. The value of the mortgage has fallen due to rising interest rates.

The potential value of the mortgage position is also affected by special clauses within the mortgage document. If the mortgage specifies that there is no penalty for prepayment, a mortgagee may elect to refinance when mortgage interest rates change significantly and pay off the higher-interest loan with a lower-interest new loan. In such cases, the potential value of the mortgage position is lost. This often happens when interest rates decrease more than 200 basis points. Generally, however, mortgagees will not pay off a fixed-rate loan if interest rates have increased, unless they sell the property. As a result, investors who acquire mortgage positions from originators and other sources often discount the value of loans at above-market interest rates in the portfolio to account for these potential conditions.

It is important to recognize that although the value of a fixed-rate mortgage may rise or fall depending on variations in interest rates, the payment schedule and outstanding balance will not be influenced by interest rate fluctuations. It is no wonder, therefore, that lenders prefer variable-rate mortgages over fixed-rate mortgages to avoid interest rate risks.

EXAMPLE 9

Consider the same situation discussed in the previous example—i.e., a $150,000 mortgage amortized monthly over 30 years at a fixed rate of 10%. What will the outstanding balance of this mortgage be after five years, assuming all payments have been made on time?

To solve this problem the appraiser uses the same procedure demonstrated in the previous problem, except the interest rate of the mortgage is applied rather than market interest rates. Using a 10% interest rate and a 25-year remaining mortgage term in the formula yields the following annuity factor:

$$
\begin{aligned}
\text{Annuity factor} \ &= \ (1 - (1 / (1 + I)^n) / I \\
&= \ (1 - (1 / (1 + 0.10/12)^{25 \times 12})) / 0.10/12 \\
&= \ (1 - (1 / (1.00833)^{300})) / 0.00833 \\
&= \ (1 - (1 / 12.04499)) / 0.00833 \\
&= \ (1 - 0.08302) / 0.00833 \\
&= \ 0.91698 / 0.00833 \\
&= \ 110.08163
\end{aligned}
$$

Applying this factor to the payment of $1,316 yields an outstanding balance of $144,867.

EXAMPLE 10

A shared appreciation mortgage (SAM) is a unique mortgage arrangement in which a lender agrees to share in the future appreciation potential of a property, generally in exchange for a lower interest rate. For example, assume a private lender has agreed to extend a $250,000 mortgage to a borrower for the acquisition of a $330,000 parcel of vacant, commercially zoned land in a rapidly developing area. The going market terms associated with such loans call for an interest rate of 10% fully amortized over 15 to 20 years. In exchange for a lower interest rate of 8.0% and a 20-year amortization schedule, the borrower has agreed to sell the property after a five-year holding period and allow the lender to share in 30% of the appreciation. What amount of appreciation must the property generate for the lender to realize a yield rate of 12%? Note, the required yield of 12% is in excess of the market yield of 10% due to the greater amount of risk present in this mortgage; the lender is sharing in the risk of appreciation, which is uncertain.

The solution to this problem involves four steps:

1. The loan payment at 8% is calculated.

2. The outstanding loan balance after five years is calculated.

3. The future value necessary to generate a yield rate of 12% is calculated.

4. The future value is divided by 30%, the share of the lender, to generate the total required property appreciation.

Solution

Applying the method of calculation demonstrated in Example 8, the monthly payment on a $250,000 loan at 8% amortized monthly for 20 years is calculated to be $2,091.

Applying the method of calculation shown in Example 9, the outstanding loan balance after five years is calculated to be $219,556.

Next the appraiser calculates the required future value needed to yield a 12% return based on a $250,000 loan, a $2,091 monthly payment, and a five-year (60-month) holding period. This basically involves calculating the future value of $250,000 at 12% for 60 months (five years) and deducting the future value of a $2,091 payment at 12% for 60 months.

The future value formula is applied as follows:

$$
\begin{aligned}
\text{Future value} \ &= \ \text{present value } (1 + I)^n \\
&= \ \$250,000 \ (1 + 0.12/12)^{5 \times 12} \\
&= \ \$250,000 \ (1.01)^{60} \\
&= \ \$250,000 \ (1.8167) \\
&= \ \$454,175
\end{aligned}
$$

The future value of an annuity is calculated as follows:

$$
\begin{aligned}
\text{Future value} \quad &= \quad \text{payment } (((1+I)^n - 1)/I) \\
&= \quad \$2{,}091\ (((1 + 0.12/12)^{5 \times 12} - 1)/0.12/12) \\
&= \quad \$2{,}091\ (((1.01)^{60} - 1)/0.01) \\
&= \quad \$2{,}091\ ((1.8167 - 1)/0.01) \\
&= \quad \$2{,}091\ (0.8167/0.01) \\
&= \quad \$2{,}091 \times 81.67 \\
&= \quad \$170{,}772
\end{aligned}
$$

Deducting the future value of the annuity payment from the future value of the loan amount yields a required future value, calculated as follows:

$$
\begin{aligned}
&\quad \$454{,}175 \\
- &\quad \$170{,}772 \\
\hline
= &\quad \$283{,}403
\end{aligned}
$$

However, of this future value, $219,556 represents the outstanding loan balance. Thus the reversion to the lender is the difference, or $63,847.

Since the lender will be receiving 30% of the appreciation of the property, the property must appreciate by approximately $212,820 ($63,846/0.3). Therefore, the property must appreciate at an overall rate of 65% ($212,820/$330,000) over five years, or 13% per year, for the lender to meet its yield requirement.

EXAMPLE 11

A participation mortgage is another specialized type of mortgage arrangement. In a participation mortgage, a lender may agree to a below-market interest rate in exchange for receiving some of the cash flows generated by the property.

For example, assume the following data pertain to a warehouse property:

Lease basis: triple net to lessor

Lease term: 10 years

Rent payment: $6,200 per month

NOI after management and reserves: $6,000 per month

Loan amount: $800,000

Market interest rate: 8%

Amortization period: 20 years, monthly

In exchange for a below-market interest rate of 6%, the lender will receive 30% of the net cash flows (0.30 x $6,000), or $1,800 per month. What is the lender's yield at this rate of participation if the agreed-upon investment holding period is 10 years?

The solution to this problem involves four steps:

1. The loan payment at 6% is calculated.

2. The outstanding loan balance after 10 years is calculated.

3. The participation cash flow is calculated.

4. The resulting yield rate is calculated.

Solution

Applying the methodologies demonstrated in previous examples, the payment on a $800,000 loan at a 6% interest rate amortized over a 20-year, monthly schedule is $5,731. The outstanding balance on this loan at the end of the 10-year investment holding period will be $516,251. The total monthly income to the lender will consist of the loan payment of $5,731 plus the participation payment of $1,800 for a total of $7,531 per month. Solving for the yield rate results in a return of 0.76% per month, or 9.12% per year. Note, this yield is higher than the market rate of 8% because above-market risk is associated with a participation mortgage.

SUMMARY

Equity and debt are forms of capital used to finance real property, and the most common debt instrument is a mortgage. Mortgages are extended to borrowers (mortgagors) by lenders (mortgagees) using property as collateral for repayment of the debt. The cost of this debt is reflected in the interest rate.

There are several types of mortgages, including first, second, and third; guaranteed, insured, and conventional; institutional and private; fixed- and variable-rate; and shared appreciation and participation, among others. The value of a fixed-rate mortgage is directly influenced by the movement of interest rates, but not the outstanding balance.

Variable-rate mortgages were developed to help protect lenders against the negative impact of potential fluctuations in interest rates. In a variable-rate mortgage, the lender shifts interest rate risk onto the borrower. To entice borrowers to accept this greater risk, the interest rate associated with variable-rate mortgages is typically lower than the rate associated with fixed-rate mortgages.

CHAPTER FIVE

LIFE ESTATES

A life estate is a unique type of partial interest. In this form of estate, a designated beneficiary, the life tenant, has the right to use and occupy a parcel of real estate for the duration of his or her life. The life tenant generally enjoys this right without any obligation to pay rent, but typically he or she must maintain the property and pay all applicable liens and taxes. The owner of a real property encumbered by a life estate is called the *remainderman*; he or she enjoys the remaining rights to the property once the life tenant is deceased. A life estate is defined as follows:

> The total rights of use, occupancy and control, limited to the lifetime of a designated party.[1]

Figure 5.1 illustrates the rights associated with a life estate.

Figure 5.1 Rights Associated with a Life Estate

Remainderman:
*Right of Future
Use and Reversion*

Life Tenant:
*Right of Use and
Occupancy for Life*

Not to scale, for illustration only

---

1. Appraisal Institute, *The Dictionary of Real Estate Appraisal,* 3d ed. (Chicago: Appraisal Institute, 1993), 207-208.

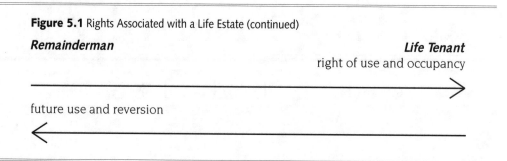

Figure 5.1 Rights Associated with a Life Estate (continued)

Remainderman   *Life Tenant*
right of use and occupancy

future use and reversion

EXAMPLE 12

Assume a client requests the appraisal of a single-family home in an older, established neighborhood. The home was previously owned free and clear by Mr. Samuel Jones, who allowed his elderly sister, Patricia Sullivan, to live in it rent free. Her only obligations were to pay all applicable taxes and liens and to maintain the property in reasonably good condition, which she has gratefully done. Last year Mr. Jones passed away and, in his will, he left the home to his son, David. However, Jones granted a life estate to his sister to provide for her welfare after his death. The client is an attorney seeking an appraisal of the property to establish David's inheritance tax liability. Thus, the client is seeking the appraisal of a property encumbered by a life estate, i.e., the remainderman's position.

Solution

There are three steps involved in estimating the value of the remainderman's interest.

1. Estimate the most likely time of death of the life tenant.

2. Forecast the future value of the property at this time.

3. Discount the forecast future value of the property over the remaining duration of the life estate at the appropriate discount rate.

To estimate the most likely time of death of a life tenant, actuarial or statistical tables relating to life expectancy are referenced. Such tables can be found at the local library and on the Internet. One such table can be found in the *Statistical Abstract of the United States*, available at most libraries and over the Internet at http://www.census.gov/ftp/pub/statab/www/ under the Vital Statistics category. Table 5.1 is an excerpt from this source.

Table 5.1 Expectation of Life in Years

| Age in 1990 | Total | White | | Black | |
		Male	Female	Male	Female
At birth	75.5	72.9	79.6	64.6	73.8
50	29.2	26.9	31.8	22.7	28.3
51	28.3	26.0	30.9	22.0	27.5
52	27.4	25.2	30.0	21.3	26.7
53	26.6	24.4	29.1	20.6	25.9
54	25.8	23.5	28.2	19.9	25.1
55	24.9	22.7	27.3	19.3	24.3
56	24.1	21.9	26.5	18.6	23.6
57	23.3	21.1	25.6	18.0	22.8
58	22.5	20.4	24.8	17.4	22.1
59	21.8	19.6	24.0	16.8	21.3
60	21.0	18.9	23.1	16.2	20.6
61	20.2	18.1	22.3	15.6	19.9
62	19.5	17.4	21.5	15.0	19.2
63	18.8	16.7	20.7	14.4	18.5
64	18.1	16.0	20.0	13.9	17.8
65	17.4	15.4	19.2	13.4	17.2
70	14.0	12.3	15.5	10.9	14.1
75	11.1	9.5	12.1	8.7	11.2
80	8.4	7.2	9.1	6.7	8.6
85 and over	6.2	5.3	6.5	5.1	6.3

Source: *Statistical Abstract of the United States, 1994*. Table No. 116.

Note that the table indicates the average life expectancy actually increases for individuals who have already had a relatively long life. At birth the average predicted life expectancy is 75.5 years. However, for those individuals who have already reached 75 years of age, the predicted life expectancy is 86 years (75 years plus 11.1 years). Thus the table is exponential, not linear. For purposes of this example, assume the life tenant is a 75-year-old white female. As such, her life expectancy is 12.1 more years, indicating a predicted age of death of approximately 87 years.

The next step is to forecast the future value of the property at the predicted date of death. This is the most subjective part of the valuation of a life estate. Many appraisers estimate this value by first estimating the current market value of the property and then adjusting for anticipated appreciation over the predicted remaining life of the tenant. For example, assuming the current value is $100,000, the predicted date of death is in 12.1 years, and the forecast rate of appreciation is 3% per year, the future value of the property would be $143,000, calculated as follows:

$$FV = PV (1 + I)^n$$

where: FV = future value of property

              PV = present (current) value of property

              I = interest rate

              n = predicted remaining life in years

Substituting numbers into the formula yields:

$$FV = \$100,000 (1 + 0.03)^{12.1}$$
$$= \$100,000 (1.03)^{12.1}$$
$$= \$100,000 (1.43)$$
$$= \$143,000$$

Once future value has been projected out at the anticipated rate of appreciation, it must be discounted back to present value. This may seem illogical, forecasting a future value and then discounting it back to present value again, especially when current value is already known. The procedure is necessary, however, because the current value of the property is an *unencumbered* value, and the appraisal assignment is to estimate an *encumbered* value— i.e., the value of a property encumbered by a life estate.

The appropriate discount rate to apply is a function of the property type, market conditions, and the expected date of death. A property in an established or growing neighborhood carries less risk than a property in a declining area that is already showing signs of blight or decay. Also, shorter life expectancies have less risk than longer life expectancies, just as the yield rate on a five-year treasury note is generally lower than the yield on a 30-year note (in periods of low inflation). In this example, the property is a single-family residence in a well-established, stable neighborhood, the remaining term is 12.1 years, and a 10% discount rate is applicable. The solution follows:

$$PV = FV/(1 + I)^n$$
$$= \$143,000/(1.10)^{12.1}$$
$$= \$143,000/3.1685$$
$$= \$45,132, \text{ or } \$45,000 \text{ rounded}$$

As can be seen, the remainderman's interest is valued at $45,000, much lower than the unencumbered fee simple value estimate of $100,000.

EXAMPLE 13

Consider the same information given in the preceding example, but now the appraisal problem is to estimate the value of the life estate, the interest enjoyed by the life tenant. Assume a survey of rent comparables reveals that the market rent for the home occupied by Patricia Sullivan would be $600 per month (if available for rent). Further research reveals rental rates are net, with the tenant responsible for utility and maintenance expenses as well as taxes and insurance. Therefore, as a result of the life estate granted her, Ms. Sullivan is currently enjoying a monthly benefit of $600. If market rents are forecast to increase at a rate of 3% per year over the remainder of her expected life, the value of her interest at a 10% discount rate can be calculated as shown in Table 5.2.

Table 5.2 Present Value of Life Estate

Year	Monthly Rent Savings	Annual Rent Savings	Present Value Factor at 10% Discount Rate	Present Value
1	$600.00	$7,200.00	0.9091	$6,545.52
2	$618.00	$7,416.00	0.8264	$6,128.58
3	$636.54	$7,638.48	0.7513	$5,738.79
4	$655.64	$7,867.68	0.6830	$5,373.63
5	$675.31	$8,103.72	0.6209	$5,031.60
6	$695.57	$8,346.84	0.5645	$4,711.79
7	$716.44	$8,597.28	0.5132	$4,412.12
8	$737.93	$8,855.16	0.4665	$4,130.93
9	$760.07	$9,120.84	0.4241	$3,868.15
10	$782.87	$9,394.44	0.3855	$3,621.56
11	$806.36	$9,676.32	0.3505	$3,391.55
12	$830.55	$9,966.60	0.3186	$3,175.36
12.1	$855.47	$1,026.56	0.3155	$323.88
				$56,453.46

The total present value of the life estate in this example is $56,453, rounded to $56,500.

SUMMARY

In a life estate a designated party enjoys the right to use and occupy a parcel of real estate for the duration of his or her life. The party who enjoys this right is called the *life tenant* and the party who holds the remaining rights in the property is called the *remainderman*. Life estates are often granted to family members as a means of providing for their welfare; they are also used in estate planning.

To estimate the value of a life estate to the remainderman, the predicted remaining life of the tenant is first estimated using actuarial/statistical tables. Then the appraiser estimates the current value of the property and forecasts its future value at the end of the tenancy period. Finally, the forecast future value is discounted to the present at an appropriate discount rate.

To estimate the value of a life estate to the beneficiary, or life tenant, the predicted remaining life of the tenant is estimated based on actuarial/statistical tables. Then the rent savings to the tenant are estimated and discounted to present value at an appropriate discount rate.

CHAPTER SIX

CONSERVATION EASEMENTS

E asements are legal divisions of real property which convey use, but not ownership. They are similar to a lease, except the real property rights are granted, not rented. One popular form of easement is the conservation easement, which is discussed in this chapter.

As the movement to conserve and protect natural resources grows, more and more appraisers are being asked to appraise conservation easements. This particular type of easement is a tool used primarily by public sector and environmental entities to conserve and preserve tracts of land in a manner that is less expensive than outright fee simple acquisition. Thus, the term "less-than-fee" is often used in conjunction with this form of easement. A conservation easement is defined as follows:

> A restriction that limits the future use of a property to
> preservation, conservation or wildlife habitat. [1]

The most common result of a conservation easement is the removal of all or some of the future development rights from the fee position so the parcel can remain in its natural, undeveloped state into perpetuity. Figure 6.1 illustrates the transfer of rights involved in a conservation easement.

In a conservation easement, development rights are typically transferred to the easement owner in exchange for compensation. As a result, the underlying property owner is left with limited uses of the property as specified in the easement.

---

1. Appraisal Institute, *The Dictionary of Real Estate Appraisal*, 3d ed. (Chicago: Appraisal Institute, 1993), 72.

Figure 6.1 Transfer of Rights in Conservation Easement

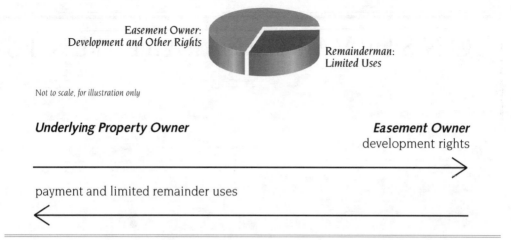

Easement Owner:
Development and Other Rights

Remainderman:
Limited Uses

Not to scale, for illustration only

Underlying Property Owner   **Easement Owner**

development rights

⟶

payment and limited remainder uses

⟵

EXAMPLE 14

The senior land resource manager of a billion-dollar timber and wood products company calls to request an appraisal. The subject property is a 25,000-acre timber tract owned by the company and strategically located near its timber processing mill. The tract is sandwiched between a state park and a national forest and enjoys extensive frontage along two, asphalt-paved county roadways. It is improved with a good network of well-maintained access trail roads, fire lines, and boundary fencing. The tract consists of approximately 80% plantable uplands and 20% Palustrine (freshwater swamp) wetlands. The uplands are planted with pine of various age classes, with nearly 75% of the inventory merchantable.

Though the subject is mostly rural, development pressures are slowly encroaching. A group of investors recently acquired a similar large parcel in the vicinity, subsequently breaking it up into smaller tracts for sale to hunt clubs, rural homesteaders, and farmers. While the subject tract is zoned for agriculture, the future land use plan recognizes that land use patterns are in transition and has designated approximately half of the property with a low-density, rural residential classification. Therefore, rezoning and subdivision of portions of the tract appears to be a legally permissible option.

The client further reports that a government agency is seeking to acquire a conservation easement over the property to preserve it into perpetuity. This agency wants to convert the tract into a wildlife preserve and a corridor for a rare species of black bear, which is found almost exclusively in the adjoining national forest (a 105,000-acre preserve). By acquiring the tract, the government hopes to bridge the gap between the state park and federal lands and provide greater roaming territory for the bears.

In response to heavy political pressure and media coverage, the client has reluctantly entered into negotiations. The company does not want to sell the tract, as it is one of the most productive in their inventory. A compromise has been proposed. If ownership of the land can be retained for timber production purposes, the company is willing to grant a conservation easement over the tract to ensure it will never be developed and thus meet the goal of preserving wildlife habitat for the bears.

In the proposed easement, the company will transfer two primary rights. First, it will grant all rights associated with future development to the government agency, while retaining the right to continue tree farming operations. Second, it will minimize clear-cut areas on the tract. (A clear-cut area is one in which all trees are removed during harvesting.) By limiting clear cuts to 1,000 acres per year, the company believes adequate tree cover and wildlife habitat will be maintained for the bears, albeit with trees in various stages of growth. Specifically, if planting and harvesting schedules are based on 1,000-acre stands and maturity, depending on soil types, climate, and planted species, is typically reached in 25 years, all the trees on the tract will be replaced every 25 years (25,000 acres /1,000 acres per year = 25 years). Though this restriction will limit the income potential of the tract, the timber company believes the production loss is worth the public relation gains to be realized.

Except for these restrictions, the timber company will retain the right to use the tract for tree farming operations into perpetuity. This includes the right to harvest, plant, maintain access trails, thin trees, and burn brush. Thus, the company is seeking to transfer only a part, or a fraction, of the rights associated with ownership. They need an appraisal to establish a sale price acceptable to both parties. This is the sale of an easement, not a lease.

Solution

Conceptually the problem is fairly simple. The appraiser must estimate the value of the development rights and the impact on value of the clear-cut restriction. In practice, finding a solution can be difficult, depending on the amount and type of market data available. In this example, a combination of the sales comparison and income approaches will be applied.

Probably the best way to estimate the value of a conservation easement is to identify recent sales of similar easements in the marketplace. Such easements are becoming more common, but they generally involve government agencies. Because government agencies and other public sector groups may have different acquisition motivations than private sector participants, special care must be taken to ensure that the governmental or quasi-governmental entity paid market value for the acquisition. Therefore, when appraising a private property interest, it is wise to avoid transactions involving government agencies unless they represent market transactions for real property interests and were not subject to condemnation. Transactions involving conservation easements among private sector parties are excellent indicators of value, should they be found.

Due to the rarity of private sector conservation easement transactions, a "before-and-after" analysis is usually performed. In the "before" analysis, the value of the tract as unencumbered is estimated. Then an "after" valuation is performed to consider the impact of the restrictions associated with the easement. Finally, the value of the easement (rights acquired) is estimated as the difference between the before and after values. If the easement encumbers only a part of the tract, severance damages to the remainder parcel may also be present. In this example, the easement will encumber the entire tract so no remainder parcel is considered.

The key to proper application of this methodology is an accurate highest and best use conclusion. In this example, the highest and best use of the parcel is changing from tree farming to recreational and residential subdivision use. This is evident from the recent sale of a similar parcel in the area acquired for these purposes. Therefore, in the before analysis, recent sales of large tracts acquired for residential and recreational subdivision are identified and researched. Assume the following comparable sales were found:

Sale	Date	Acres	Motivation	Price/Acre*
1	05/94	15,000	Residential and timber uses	$500
2	06/95	22,000	Residential, recreation and timber uses	$450
3	07/96	29,000	Residential, recreation and timber uses	$400

* Land value only, excluding value contribution of timber.

In preparing the table, the timber value was extracted from each sale to yield the allocated land value. This is an important step because the conservation easement being appraised does not include the acquisition of any timber. All timber will remain in the ownership of the timber company. The easement pertains solely to development rights and clear-cut restrictions which limit the land's *future* harvesting potential.

Based on the sales provided and considering the size and other features of the subject tract, a unit value of $425 per acre is considered reasonable. Therefore, the before value is estimated as follows:

25,000 acres x $425 per acre = $10,625,000

In the after analysis, the value of the tract as encumbered must be estimated. Here again the key is to identify sales with a similar highest and best use—parcels acquired solely for tree farming, not for imminent transition to more intense uses. Assume the following comparable sales were identified for the after analysis:

Sale	Date	Acres	Motivation	Price/Acre*
1	02/94	19,000	Tree farming	$425
2	09/95	24,000	Tree farming	$375
3	12/96	31,000	Tree farming	$325

* Land value only, excluding value contribution of timber.

Based on these sales, a value of approximately $350 per acre, or $8,750,000, appears reasonable.

An easement value of at least $75 per acre, or $1,875,000, appears reasonable based on the difference between the $425 per acre before value and the $350 per acre after value. However, this represents only part of the rights being appraised, i.e., the development rights. The rights associated with the clear-cut restriction have yet to be valued.

Assume no sales with limited clear-cut areas could be identified. Lacking such data, a creative approach must be employed. To consider the impact of clear-cut areas, the appraiser could make use of the research and computer simulation data reported in forestry trade journals. *Forest Science, The Canadian Journal of Forest Resources*, and other journals contain research articles on such topics. Another excellent way to gather data is to survey timber company managers in the area and ask their opinion as to how limiting clear-cut areas affects harvesting potential. Some may have performed their own studies on the subject.

Assume for this example that the forest resource journals and a survey of local timber companies indicate a probable reduction of 10% to 15% in the income-producing ability of the property will result from limiting clear-cut areas to 1,000 acres per year. Thus, a 12% loss in value appears reasonable. This deduction applies to the tree farming use value of the property because the ratios estimated from the forestry sources apply to timber tracts, not development tracts. Therefore, the loss in value associated with clear-cut restrictions is estimated at approximately $42 per acre (12% x $350 per acre). The total "after" value is estimated as follows:

Tree farming use value—25,000 acres x $350/acre	$8,750,000
Loss in value due to clear-cut restrictions—	
25,000 acres x $42/acre	– 1,050,000
After valuation	$7,700,000

The total value of the easement is estimated as follows:

	Before value
−	After value
=	Value of easement

Inserting figures produces these calculations

	$10,625,000
−	$ 7,700,000
=	$ 2,925,000, or $117 per acre

If the easement buyer were also interested in acquiring hunting rights or limiting the types of persons able to access the tract, then additional computations to determine compensation would be necessary. For example, if the acquiring entity wanted to eliminate hunting on the property, and the timber company was leasing the property to a hunt club for $5 per acre, or $125,000, the capitalized value of this loss in income would also be considered.

SUMMARY

Easements are a form of legal division of real property. A conservation easement is a tool employed by the public sector, environmental groups, and other parties to conserve and preserve real property in a manner that is less expensive than outright fee simple acquisition. Due to their lower cost, conservation easements are becoming increasingly popular. The most common result of a conservation easement is the removal of all future development rights from the fee position so the parcel can remain in its natural, undeveloped state into perpetuity.

In estimating the value of a conservation easement or the value of a property encumbered by such an easement, all three approaches to value can be applied. The applicability of each approach is a function of the problem at hand and the market data available.

CHAPTER SEVEN

TRANSFERABLE DEVELOPMENT RIGHTS

T he concept of transferable development rights (TDRs) emerged from the growth management and land planning movement of the 1960s and 1970s. In an effort to mitigate traffic congestion, strained utility capacity, inadequate open/recreational space, and other infrastructure deficiencies, many local and state governments adopted future land use plans and growth management strategies to control the huge social cost associated with urban sprawl and inner-city neglect. Before such policies were implemented, most developers weren't burdened (or concerned) with the long-term costs of development, such as the construction and maintenance of water and sewer facilities, roads, schools, and parks and the provision of police, fire, rescue, and other necessary services to end users. Instead, developers were typically free to focus on subdividing tracts of land into lots, developing and selling the lots, and then moving on to the next project, leaving long-term costs for end users and government entities.

However, rapid suburban growth and the resultant inner-city decay spread funds too thin for government to continue to bear this cost burden alone. Thus, a movement towards land use control and cost-sharing was born. One land use and growth management tool often employed is the transferable development right, defined as follows:

> A development right that is separated from a landowner's
> bundle of rights and transferred, generally by sale, to another
> landowner in the same or a different area. [1]

---

1. Appraisal Institute, *The Appraisal of Real Estate,* 11th ed. (Chicago: Appraisal Institute, 1996), 148.

Government initiated this concept to ensure that adequate infrastructure and provisions for the cost sharing of public services are in place before development begins.

For example, a development area may consist of a designated large parcel or group of parcels allocated a particular set of development rights, which indicates that sufficient infrastructure capacity and access to public services exist to serve the needs of potential consumers or occupants of the designated area. The owner/developer can then sell or consume these development rights; they become a marketable commodity which can be separated from a particular parcel, but must be limited to the designated development area.

For example, assume a 1,000-acre tract has been allocated development rights for 1,000 homes, 100,000 square feet of retail space, and 75,000 square feet of office space. As individual parcels within this 1,000-acre development area are sold, development rights corresponding with the type of use intended for the site are also transferred. When all development rights in the project are sold, no more development can take place, even if there are remainder parcels (unsold parcels). Thus, rights may or may not be tied to individual parcels.

Figure 7.1 illustrates the transfer of rights when a site has development rights.

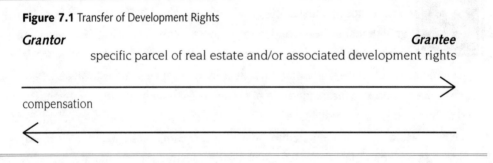

Figure 7.1 Transfer of Development Rights

Grantor   *Grantee*

specific parcel of real estate and/or associated development rights

compensation

Note that the transfer may not include any real estate, just development rights. If a developer has sold a 10-acre site and 50,000 square feet of office rights to an office user and the office user later wants to expand his facility without acquiring any more land, the developer can sell him additional development rights exclusive of additional real estate. Figure 7.2 illustrates this situation.

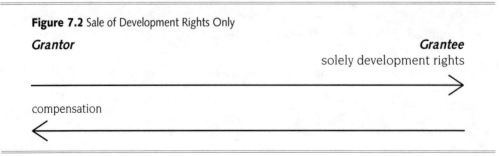

Figure 7.2 Sale of Development Rights Only

Grantor   *Grantee*

solely development rights

compensation

Transfers of development rights may or may not be linked to a particular parcel of real estate.

EXAMPLE 15

A developer has undertaken a large project known as Eagle Landing and has borne the cost of obtaining permits and developing the roads, sidewalks, parks, and open space associated with the project. He has also shared in long-term costs by dedicating a parcel of land within the community as a site for future development of an elementary school and has paid nearly $2,000,000 in partnership fees with local government to construct a new water and sewer facility. In exchange, the county has granted Eagle Landing the following development rights:

Development area: 2,500 acres

Single-family residential: 1,000 units

Multifamily residential: 250 units

Office space: 100,000 square feet

Retail/commercial space: 300,000 square feet

Industrial space: none

Parks and open areas: 200 acres (to include a 130-acre, 18-hole golf course)

Eagle Landing is now in its fifth year of operation with build-out projected at 10 years. A golf course, two parks, 500 homes, a 200,000-sq.-ft. shopping center, and 25,000 square feet of office space have been constructed.

One day a local banker calls to request the appraisal of a 55,000-sq.-ft. site to be developed with a proposed, 8,000-sq.-ft., multitenant professional office building. The site is located within the Eagle Landing office park and has been allocated 8,000 square feet of office development rights. The appraisal problem in this case is to estimate the market value of the site and associated development rights.

Solution

In appraising transferable development rights, the best methodology to apply is the sales comparison approach. The cost and income approaches can also be useful indicators of value in a residual application (see Example 17).

The sales comparison approach is generally the most straightforward valuation methodology and the easiest to understand. Assume for this example that market research reveals three other recent transfers of sites with office development rights within Eagle Landing as shown in the following table.

Sale	Date	Price	Parcel Size in Square Feet	Square Feet of TDRs	Price/ Sq. Ft.	Price/TDR
1	03/17/96	$ 75,000	30,000	5,000	$2.50	$15.00
2	07/23/96	$195,000	100,000	15,000	$1.95	$13.00
3	11/01/96	$ 84,000	40,000	6,000	$2.10	$14.00

As can be seen, the comparable sales are all recent and range in size from 30,000 to 100,000 square feet of land area and from 5,000 to 15,000 square feet of TDRs. The indicated units of comparison range from $1.95 to $2.50 per square foot of site area and from $13.00 to $15.00 per square foot of TDRs. It is important to recognize that these sales represent the transfer of both land and specific rights to develop the land. Therefore, both units of comparison are relevant indicators of value.

The subject site contains 55,000 square feet of site area and has been allocated 8,000 square feet of TDRs. An analysis of the sales reveals that size is the primary factor influencing the value range in this case. Sorting the sales by size yields the following value schedule:

Sale	Date	Price	Parcel Size in Square Feet	Square Feet of TDRs	Price/ Sq. Ft.	Price/TDR
1	03/17/96	$ 75,000	30,000	5,000	$2.50	$15.00
3	11/01/96	$ 84,000	40,000	6,000	$2.10	$14.00
Subject			55,000	8,000	?	?
2	07/23/96	$195,000	100,000	15,000	$1.95	$13.00

It appears that the value of the subject property would fall within the range established by Sales 2 and 3. Specifically, a value greater than $1.95 but less than $2.10 per square foot of site area, and a value greater than $13.00 but less than $14.00 per square foot of TDRs would be reasonable. The concluded value is estimated as follows:

Land value analysis:

    55,000 square feet x $2.00 per square foot $110,000

TDR value analysis:

    8,000 square feet x $13.75 per square foot $110,000

This sales comparison approach methodology can be adapted to situations in which there is no sales history within the subject development area, but the results will be less accurate.

EXAMPLE 16

Consider the same general information presented in the preceding example, but assume that there is no sales history within the subject development area. When a better source of data is lacking, recent sales of office building sites in comparable areas can be identified and then analyzed based on price per square foot of building area. The comparable sales described below were analyzed.

Sale 1 is a 45,000-sq.-ft. site which was sold on January 10, 1996, for $100,000. It is located in a small office park approximately two miles east of the subject park and, subsequent to acquisition, was developed with a 7,000-sq.-ft., multitenant office building.

Sale 2 is a 25,000-sq.-ft. site which was sold on April 2, 1996, for $70,000. It is located in the same small office park as Sale 1 and, subsequent to acquisition, was developed with a 4,500-sq.- ft. office building.

Sale 3 is a 120,000-sq.-ft. site which was sold on October 21, 1996, for $240,000. It is in a small office park approximately five miles north of the subject park and, subsequent to acquisition, was developed with a 24,000-sq.-ft. office building.

The units of comparison extracted from these sales follow:

Sale	Date	Price	Parcel Size in Square Feet	Square Feet of Office Space	Price/ Sq. Ft. Land	Price/ Sq. Ft. Office
1	01/10/96	$ 100,000	45,000	7,000	$2.22	$14.29
2	04/02/96	$ 70,000	25,000	4,500	$2.80	$15.56
3	10/21/96	$ 240,000	120,000	24,000	$2.00	$10.00

The comparable sales range in unit price from $2.00 to $2.80 per square foot of site area, and from $10.00 to $15.56 per square foot of office area. Analysis of the sales reveals that all were located in newly developed office parks in growing areas and the primary factor influencing the value range is size. Sorting the sales by size and inserting the subject property in the analysis yields the following table:

Sale	Date	Price	Parcel Size in Square Feet	Square Feet of Office Space	Price/ Sq. Ft. Land	Price/ Sq. Ft. Office
2	04/02/96	$ 70,000	25,000	4,500	$2.80	$15.56
1	01/10/96	$ 100,000	45,000	7,000	$2.22	$14.29
Subject			55,000	8,000	?	?
3	10/21/96	$ 240,000	120,000	24,000	$2.00	$10.00

It appears reasonable to estimate that the indicated unit value of the subject property would be greater than $2.00 but less than $2.22 per square foot of site area, and greater than $10.00 but less than $14.29 per square foot of office area. The following value estimate is concluded

Land value analysis:

55,000 square feet x $2.10 per square foot	$115,500

TDR value analysis:

8,000 square feet x $14.00 per square foot	$112,000

EXAMPLE 17

When insufficient sales data in the region make the sales comparison approach inapplicable, a residual analysis employing the income and cost approaches can be applied as additional support for the value conclusion. Consider once again the subject site with 55,000 square feet of area and 8,000 square feet of office development rights. Now assume that there have been no sales in the subject office park and no sales of vacant office sites in the region. To solve a TDR problem such as this without comparable sales data, the appraiser estimates the prospective value of the property when complete using the income approach and then deducts the cost of development and profit to yield the residual value of the land and the associated development rights.

The first step in the analysis is to estimate the prospective value of the property (as if developed) via the income approach. The appraiser does this by estimating the income earning potential of the proposed 8,000-sq.-ft. office building and then deducting a market allowance for vacancy and collection loss along with operating expenses to yield the building's estimated net operating income. This income is capitalized (or discounted) into an indication of value.

Assume that the proposed 8,000-sq.-ft. office building has been pre-leased as a branch office of a national insurance company with an A+ credit rating. The tenant has agreed to a 10-year lease with renewal options at a contract rent of $13.50 per square foot, triple net, with escalations tied to increases in the Consumer Price Index (CPI). Net operating income is estimated as follows:

Contract rent:

8,000 sq. ft. x $13.50/sq. ft.	$108,000
Less allowance for vacancy and collection loss @ 1% *	1,080
Effective gross income	$106,920

* Low allowance reflects good credit rating of tenant and long lease term.

Less operating expenses:

Management @ 3%	3,208
Reserves @ $0.25/sq. ft.	2,000
Net operating income	$101,712

Market research reveals the applicable capitalization rate is 9.5%, so the value of the proposed development when completed is projected as follows:

$$\$101,712 / 0.095 = \$1,070,653$$
Rounded to $1,070,000

The appraiser's next step is to research cost guides, cost comparables, and other sources of proposed construction cost data to estimate the reproduction cost of the improvements. Assume the following cost data are gathered:

Office building:

8,000 square feet x $85.00/sq. ft.	$680,000
Parking lot, landscaping, and signage	100,000
Miscellaneous costs	25,000
Subtotal	$805,000
Add 20% developer's profit incentive	161,000
Total cost	$966,000

Thus, assuming this project is financially feasible, the residual value of the site and associated development rights is estimated as follows:

	Income approach value
−	Cost to develop
=	Residual value

Inserting numbers yields,

$$\begin{array}{r} \$1,070,000 \\ - \quad \$966,000 \\ \hline = \quad \$104,000 \end{array}$$

Note, this residual value includes the value of both the land and TDRs.

EXAMPLE 18

All the previous examples in this chapter have included both land and development rights. What happens if no land is being transferred, just development rights? Consider the same 55,000-sq.-ft. site, but now assume that the office developer wants to construct a 5,000-sq.-ft. addition to the 8,000-sq.-ft. office building. There is sufficient land area remaining to support the addition, but the site and original acquisition included only 8,000 square feet of development rights. Therefore, the local building department will not approve the plan unless 5,000 square feet of additional office development rights are acquired. What is the value of these additional development rights?

For this example, assume market research reveals the following sales of office development rights, exclusive of land area. All of the sales are within the Eagle Landing development area.

Sale	Date	Price	Square Feet of Office TDR	Price/Sq. Ft. of Office TDR
1	05/21/96	$ 48,000	4,800	$10.00
Subject		?	5,000	?
2	10/11/96	$58,500	6,500	$ 9.00
3	12/27/96	$36,000	3,000	$12.00

The sales of the office TDRs range from $9.00 to $12.00 per square foot, exclusive of land, and it appears that size is the primary factor influencing the value range. Recognizing that the problem involves 5,000 square feet of office TDRs, a value within the range appears reasonable. Applying a unit value of $9.75 per square foot yields the following value estimate:

Office building TDR

5,000 sq. ft. x $9.75/sq. ft. = $48,750

Note that this value is lower than the combined land and office development rights value estimated at approximately $14.00 per square foot in Examples 15 and 16. The difference can be attributed to the incremental value of the land above and beyond the right to develop the land. In many cases, however, there may not be any extractable land premium.

If no sales of comparable TDRs are available in the area, the problem of appraising rights separate from land becomes trickier. A combination of the income and cost approaches could be applied to extract the land value component, which would than be adjusted to separate out the development rights. This is probably the most logical method of analysis, but without market sales data, a good deal of careful reasoning and judgment would be required.

SUMMARY

Transferable development rights (TDRs) were created in the 1960s and 1970s to facilitate future land use planning and growth management and to control urban sprawl. TDRs are generally linked to, and transferable within, a designated development area. These rights may or may not be sold in conjunction with a parcel of real estate. They are both divisible and transferable, and they pose of unique fractional interest problem for real estate appraisers.

Typically the best indicator of value for TDRs is the sales comparison approach. To apply this approach, recent sales of TDRs are identified, researched, and analyzed in comparison to the subject rights. When such sales are lacking, sales of sites acquired for similar development purposes can be used or a residual analysis employing the income and cost approaches can be applied.

CHAPTER EIGHT

FRACTIONAL INTERESTS

A nother legal division of real property pertains to forms of ownership. If multiple owners are involved in a parcel of real property, then each necessarily owns a fraction of the whole. Thus, the term *fractional interest* is often used in association with multiple ownerships, such as tenancy by the entirety, joint tenancy, tenancy in common, and community property. Tenancy, in this case, is not the right associated with a lease, but refers to the form of ownership involved.

Tenancy by the entirety is a form of co-ownership enjoyed by married couples. It is, "an estate held by a husband and wife in which neither has a disposable interest in the property during the lifetime of the other, except through joint action."[1] The interesting thing about tenancy by the entirety is that the law does not recognize individual actions associated with this form of multiple ownership, just joint action. As such, if property is owned by a married couple, one spouse cannot sell the property without the cooperation of the other spouse. The married couple is legally viewed as one unit, not two. If an interest holder (one spouse) dies, then the other interest holder (the surviving spouse) automatically absorbs the interest of the deceased.

Joint tenancy and tenancy in common are multiple ownership interests outside a marriage relationship. The primary difference between these two forms of ownership is that joint tenancy, like tenancy by the entirety and community property, includes the right of survivorship while tenancy in common doesn't. If the owner of a joint tenancy interest dies, his or her interest is absorbed by the surviving owners. For this reason, many family-owned real properties are held in joint tenancy.

---

1. Appraisal Institute, *The Appraisal of Real Estate*, 11th ed. (Chicago: Appraisal Institute, 1996), 139.

Community property is defined as "property acquired by either spouse during their marriage, excluding gifts or inheritances, which belongs to them as a unit and not individually. The death of either person results in full ownership for the other." [2] This concept, like tenancy by the entirety, is linked to the marriage relationship between owners. In this case it pertains to property acquired after a marriage takes place.

Subforms of fractional interests include condominium, timeshare, real estate investment trust (REIT), limited partnerships, and corporation (business share) ownership, among others. These are referred to as subforms because they can be owned by primary forms, e.g., a condominium interest may be owned in tenancy by the entirety or a portion of a corporation may be owned in tenancy in common.

A condominium is a form of fractional ownership defined as "a multiunit structure or property in which persons hold fee simple title to individual units and an undivided interest in common areas." [3] In condominium ownership individual units are owned separately, with ownership including an undivided interest in all common areas of the project. Undivided rights, in this case, means a right in all the common areas; if the rights were divided, then they would apply only to parts of the common areas. Common areas typically include the underlying land, amenities, exterior walls and roof, interior hallways and corridors, and parking areas. Condominium owners are generally responsible for the full real estate tax, insurance, and maintenance expenses of their individual units and for a pro rata share of the expenses associated with common areas.

Timesharing is a form of fractional ownership which became popular during the 1970s and 1980s as developers attempted to expand the market for their projects (typically condominiums) to part-time and vacation-use buyers. Timesharing is defined as:

> Limited ownership interests in, or the rights of use and occupancy of, residential apartments, [condominiums] or hotel rooms. There are two forms of timesharing—fee timeshares and nonfee timeshares. Fee timeshares may be based on timeshare ownership or interval ownership. There are three types of nonfee timeshares; a prepaid lease arrangement, a vacation license, and a club membership. [4] (Bracketed insertion is the author's.)

2. Appraisal Institute, *The Dictionary of Real Estate Appraisal*, 3rd ed. (Chicago: Appraisal Institute, 1993), 66.
3. Ibid., 71.
4. Ibid., 369.

In the most common form of timeshare, the fee timeshare, an owner buys an interest in a project and receives a deed. This interest can be mortgaged, sold, leased, exchanged, willed, and assessed. In contrast, a nonfee timeshare does not involve a deed, but is basically a form of lease, temporary license, or club membership conveying the temporary right of use and occupancy in exchange for payment.

Sometimes real property is held in partnership, a form of business entity. In a general partnership, "all partners share in investment gains and losses, and each has personal and unlimited responsibility for all liabilities." [5] Some special forms of partnerships, however, limit the liability of partners. Specifically, a limited partnership is classified as a passive, nonmanaging form of ownership in which each limited partner's liability cannot exceed the amount of capital invested. In such an arrangement, a general partner manages the investment and holds unlimited liability.

Real estate investment trusts (REITs) have made a big comeback in recent years, rising out of the capital crunch of the early 1990s. REITs are a special form of business entity involved in real property investment. They are defined as follows:

> A corporation or trust that combines the capital of many investors to acquire or provide financing for all forms of real estate. A REIT serves much like a mutual fund for real estate. Its shares are freely traded, often on a major stock exchange. To qualify for the favorable tax treatment currently accorded such trusts, 95% of the taxable income of a REIT must be distributed among its shareholders, who must number at least 100 investors; no fewer than five investors can own more than 50% of the value of the REIT. The Federal Securities and Exchange Commission (SEC) stipulates that REITS with over 300 investors have to make their financial statements public. [6]

Stock corporations often own real property. Like REITS, they are business entities, but stock corporations differ in their organization and tax treatment. A stock corporation is defined as:

5. Ibid., 157.
6. Ibid., 293.

> A common legal entity in which investors provide organiza-
> tional capital by subscribing to shares that represent owner-
> ship and a right to all proprietary benefits, but are subject to
> the prior claims of operating expenses and debt service on
> capital raised by selling bonds, debentures, and other money
> market instruments. [7]

Stock corporations are not subject to the same distribution requirements as REITs and do not enjoy the same favorable tax treatment.

When ownership in real property is held via a share or interest in a partnership, stock corporation, REIT, or other business entity, the interest is held indirectly, i.e., channeled through the business entity. This is an important distinction to recognize because indirect ownership involves business ownership, and an appraisal of an indirect interest involves business valuation.

Sometimes fractional interests take the form of minority and majority interests. A minority interest is a nonmanaging interest, while a majority interest is a managing interest. Majority and minority positions have a significant influence on the value of the interest. Majority interests are more valuable than minority interests because they enjoy greater investment control and managerial influence.

The concept of fractional interests is illustrated in Figure 8.1. The pie graph shows a joint tenancy situation in which each owner enjoys a 25% interest in an estate.

Figure 8.1 Joint Tenancy

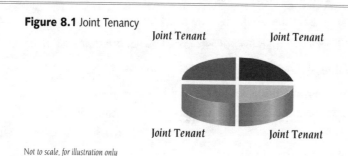

Joint Tenant   Joint Tenant

Joint Tenant   Joint Tenant

Not to scale, for illustration only

In contrast, Figure 8.2 illustrates a majority and minority division of interests.

---

7. Ibid., 350.

Figure 8.2 Majority and Minority Interests

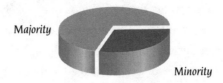

Majority

Minority

Not to scale, for illustration only

Fractional interests are often plagued with disagreements among owners, especially if one owner wants to sell and others don't. The law recognizes such situations and provides the right of partition for nonbusiness forms of ownership. Under this right, an owner of an interest can force the sale of a property or his interest in order to dissolve the relationship and cash out.

When appraising a fractional ownership interest, it is important to recognize that such interests typically sell at a discount. The discount is generally applied to reflect, among other characteristics, the interest's illiquidity; the cost, uncertainty, and time delays associated with partition; and, in the case of minority fractional interests, a lack of control and managerial power.

For example, a 25% interest in a fee simple estate held by a tenant in common will not generally sell for 25% of the market value of the property. Instead, it will most likely sell at a discount. As a result, appraising a fractional interest is not as easy as estimating the value of a particular estate and then applying a pro rata allocation.

Since most appraisals of a fractional interest are associated with tax or partition proceedings, appraisers should be aware of some prominent legal cases involving these types of interests. One of the first and most significant is *Propstra v. United States*.

John A. Propstra v. United States, 680 F.2d 1248, 1251 (9th Cir. 1982), was a dispute involving the amount of discount applicable to an undivided one-half interest in several parcels of real estate held as community property. This was an appellate case. In the lower courts, the amount of discount applied was 15% (i.e., the value of the one-half interest equaled 85% of 50% of the value of the overall property). However, the defendant, the United States (IRS), argued that no discount was applicable. The case was argued in 1981 and decided in 1982, with the appellate court upholding the lower court discount stating "because the undisputed evidence indicates that the value of the interest held by the estate was less than that interest's proportionate value of the whole, we affirm the grant of summary judgment in favor of the estate (plaintiff)." This judgment created a precedent for the discounting of fractional interests.

In the *Estate of Edgar A. Berg v. Commissioner of Internal Revenue* (976 F. 2d 1163, 8th Cir.

1992), another important judgment relating to fractional interests was made. In this case, submitted on May 14, 1992, the estate of Berg appealed a lower court decision relating to the amount of discount applied to the estate's shares in a closely held real estate holding corporation. The estate of Berg wanted a 60% discount, while the IRS argued for a 30% discount. The appellate court decided in October 1992 to uphold the lower court ruling that a 30% discount was reasonable, allocated as a 20% discount for minority interest status and a 10% discount for illiquidity.

Samuel J. LeFrak and Ethel LeFrak v. Commissioner (66 T.C.M. 1297; 1993) resulted in another important decision relating to fractional interests. This case was similar to the Berg case in that a 20% minority interest discount and 10% illiquidity discount were applied. The judge agreed that a discount of a fractional interest was applicable for the lack of control (minority status); illiquidity; and cost, uncertainty, and time delays associated with the act of partition. His opinion also included the following statement of importance:

> ...we must remind the parties that the amount of discount
> must be decided on the basis of the record in the instant
> case, and not on what a court found reasonable in another
> case involving different evidence.

Appraisers should recognize that discounts associated with the valuation of fractional interests are legally upheld, but the amount of discount must be proven on a case-by-case basis, not simply applied as precedent. This ruling places the burden to prove the applicable discount on appraisers and other expert witnesses. As with all discount rates, the applicable discount is a function of the interest type, property type, market conditions, and other factors.

The best way to estimate the applicable discount is to extract it from an analysis of sales of fractional interests in comparable properties in the area. To perform such a study, the price for which the interest was sold, the percent of ownership represented, and the overall value of the real property asset must be known. Then the actual sale price can be compared with the percent allocation of the overall property value to extract the discount as follows:

Discount = 1 − (price of fractional interest sold/pro rata percent of
interest in overall property)

For example, assume a 25% interest held in tenancy in common was sold for $175,000 and the overall value of the property was $1,000,000. The applicable discount is calculated as follows:

Discount rate	=	1 – ($175,000/($1,000,000 x 25%))
	=	1 – ($175,000/$250,000)
	=	1 – 0.7
	=	0.3, or 30%

Extracting a discount rate this way is very difficult and time-consuming and there may not be sufficient local market data to support such an analysis. The legal cases discussed above have shown that alternative methods of estimating the applicable discount are acceptable.

To quantify the amount of discount associated with a minority interest, the discounts associated with the sale of minority shares of REITs and real estate limited partnership interests can be analyzed. Specifically, the trading price of a REIT share or limited partnership interest is researched and compared with the pro rata allocation of the share (or interest) as part of the reported net asset value of the entity, which is typically reported in financial statements. The appropriate discount is then extracted as follows:

Share price of REIT (or limited partnership interest)

Compared with:

	Net asset value of REIT (or partnership)
÷	Total number of shares outstanding (partnership interests)
=	Net asset value per share (or per interest)

The applicable discount equals: 1 – (price per share/net asset value per share)

For example, assume a REIT is trading at $7.75 per share, the net asset value of the REIT is reported to be $10,000,000, and there are 1,000,000 shares outstanding. The minority (noncontrolling) discount is extracted as follows:

	Share price = $7.75	
	Net asset value	$10,000,000
÷	Total shares	1,000,000
=	Net asset value per share	$10.00

Discount	=	1 – ($ 7.75/$10.00)
	=	1 – 0.78
	=	0.22, or 22%

In this example, the minority interest discount extracted was 22%. Several different REITs, preferably made up of real estate investments similar to the subject property, should be analyzed in this way to establish a range of probable discounts.

While a share in a REIT or a limited partnership interest represents a minority interest in real estate, the subject interest being appraised may differ, e.g., it may consist of a 50% interest held in joint tenancy. REIT shares are typically liquid and are easily bought and sold on the open market, whereas a 50% stake in a property held in joint tenancy is relatively illiquid. As such, many appraisers believe that the discounts associated with limited partnerships are better indicators than those associated with REITs. A good source for discount information relating to limited partnerships is *The Partnership Spectrum*, published by Partnership Profiles, Inc. of Dallas, Texas.

In addition to discounts associated with minority status and lack of business control, discounts may also be applicable for illiquidity and the costs, time delays, and uncertainty associated with partition. Fractional interests have less marketability than sole interests due to fewer buyers, sellers, and brokers. They are much less liquid and difficult to convert to ready cash. The most likely purchasers of fractional interests are the other owners of the property. If no agreement can be reached, however, the seller may have to discount the selling price in order to attract an outside investor. If no investor can be found, the owner may have to resort to the right of partition, which means legal costs, time delays, and greater price/value uncertainty. Thus, the cost of partition is often analyzed to estimate the discount applicable.

To exercise the right of partition, the fractional interest holder petitions the court for the sale of his or her interest in an equitable manner. In granting such a request, the court may order a sale at auction, with the net proceeds distributed among the buyers according to their pro rata interests, or the court may divide a property (e.g., in the case of vacant land) among the owners.

EXAMPLE 19

The subject of the proposed analysis is an undivided fractional interest in a 5,000-sq.-ft., stand-alone retail building leased on a long-term basis to a national video rental chain. The property is an outparcel of a power shopping center fronting a major, six-lane traffic artery directly across from a regional mall. It is a Class C, good-quality structure with adequate parking developed five years ago and leased for a term of 20 years. The rental rate during the first 10-year term was a flat rate of $15.00 per square foot, triple net. The rent for the second ten-year term will be a flat rate of $20.00 per square foot, also triple net.

The attorney reports that the property was previously owned in joint tenancy by five investors, each of whom owned a 20% interest. He is representing the estate of one of the investors, who recently died. The function of the appraisal is twofold. First, the attorney requires an estimate of the market value of the estate's interest in the property for IRS tax-reporting purposes. Second, he needs an estimate of market value because the survivors are seeking to convert the interest into cash.

Solution

The first step in solving a fractional interest valuation problem is to estimate the value of the sole interest in the estate being appraised. In this case, the value of the leased fee estate in the retail building is estimated. Based on the information provided, the lease includes five more years of rent at $15.00 per square foot and then 10 years of rent at $20.00 per square foot, triple net. Assume the discount rate is estimated at 11% and the future reversionary value of the leased fee estate in 15 years is forecast at $375,000. The value of the leased fee estate is estimated in Table 8.1.

Annual rent, Years 6 - 10 : $75,000

Annual rent, Years 11 - 20 : $100,000

Forecast reversion: $375,000

Discount rate : 11%

Table 8.1 Estimated Value of Leased Fee Estate

Year of Lease	Rent/Reversion	PV Factor @ 11%	Present Value
6	$75,000	0.9009	$67,568
7	75,000	0.8116	60,870
8	75,000	0.7312	54,840
9	75,000	0.6587	49,403
10	75,000	0.5935	44,513
11	100,000	0.5346	53,460
12	100,000	0.4817	48,170
13	100,000	0.4339	43,390
14	100,000	0.3909	39,090
15	100,000	0.3522	35,220
16	100,000	0.3173	31,730
17	100,000	0.2858	28,580
18	100,000	0.2575	25,750
19	100,000	0.2320	23,200
20	100,000	0.2090	20,900
20	375,000	0.2090	$78,375
			$705,059

Thus, the value of the leased fee estate is estimated to be $705,059, rounded to $700,000. A 20% fractional interest in this estate, before discounting, would equal approximately $140,000.

Assume that market research reveals three comparable sales of fractional interests reflecting discounts of 25% to 35%. Research reports reveal that limited partnership interests are selling at discounts of 15% to 20%. A knowledgeable attorney estimates that the partition process will result in potential legal fees of $10,000 (7% of the nondiscounted value of the interest) and take up to 6 months (present value factor of 6 months at 11% APR = 0.9467, or approximately 5%). Based on the information given in this example, it appears a discount in the range of 27% to 32% would be reasonable considering the property type, tenant credit rating, minority interest, illiquidity, and other factors. This discount is estimated as follows:

Minority interest discount	15% to 20%
Illiquidity discount	12%
Total discount	27% to 32%

Thus, the value of the interest can be estimated as follows:

$$V = \$140,000 \times (1 - 0.32) = \$95,200$$
$$V = \$140,000 \times (1 - 0.27) = \$102,200$$

A reconciled value of $100,000 appears reasonable.

SUMMARY

In summary, fractional interests represent the legal division of real property, with each fraction representing a part of the whole. There are four basic forms of fractional interests: tenancy by the entirety, community property, joint tenancy, and tenancy in common. There are also many subforms, including condominium, timeshare, cooperative, partnership, REIT, and stock ownership. The valuation of each of these fractional interests presents unique problems for appraisers.

The valuation of a fractional interest will most likely require discounting the pro rata allocated value of the estate involved. A discount is applied to account for illiquidity (reduced marketability as a result of fewer buyers, sellers, and brokers); minority status, if applicable (lack of control and management of the investment); and the cost, time delay, and uncertainty associated with partition (a court action to dissolve a fractional interest ownership and compensate owners in an equitable manner). The applicable discount rate can be estimated based on 1) analysis of sales of similar interests in the local market; 2) studies of the discount associated with the sale of REIT and limited partnership interests; and 3) the estimated costs and time delays associated with the act of partition. Other factors may also be considered in estimating the discount applicable to a fractional interest in comparison to the value of the sole estate.

CHAPTER NINE

PHYSICAL INTERESTS

I n addition to divisions based on income and legal interests, real property can be divided into physical interests. The most fundamental physical divisions of property are horizontal and vertical. Horizontal divisions are primarily a result of subdivision or assemblage. In the subdivision process, a large parcel is divided into smaller parts; assemblage involves gathering together small parts to form a new, larger whole. Figures 9.1 and 9.2 illustrate the subdivision process. The assemblage process is the reverse.

Figure 9.1 Property Before Subdivision

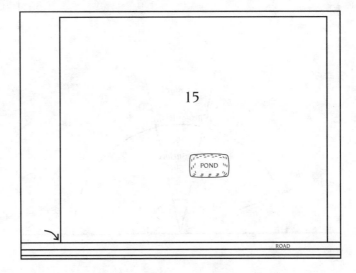

Figure 9.1 shows a tract before subdivision. Figure 9.2 shows the same tract subdivided into smaller residential lots.

Figure 9.2 Property After Subdivision

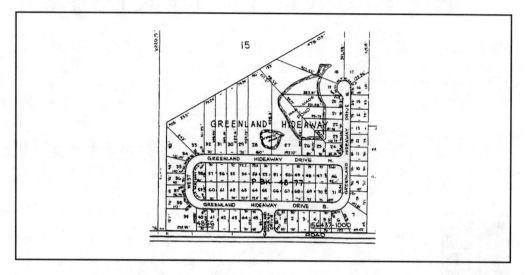

Vertical divisions of real property are perpendicular to horizontal divisions and include various surface, subsurface, and above-surface (air) rights. The concept of vertical interests is illustrated in Figure 9.3.

Figure 9.3 Vertical Interests

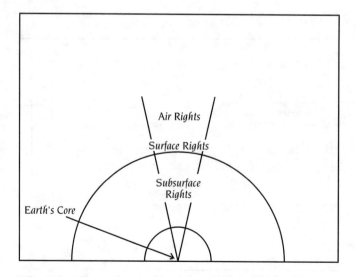

As can be seen, the surface area represents only a small portion of the vertical interests present in real property. Any use of the subsurface or air rights can have a significant impact on the use and value of the remaining estate.

Most appraisers are experienced in estimating the discounts associated with subdivision valuation and the potential plottage value associated with assemblage. However, appraisal problems involving vertical interests are less common. Therefore, this chapter will focus on an appraisal problem involving the valuation of a vertical interest.

EXAMPLE 20

The appraisal problem involves an office building located along prime riverfront property in the central business district (CBD) of a small city. The office building, a 10-story, 100,000-sq.-ft., Class A structure, offers some of the finest views in town. It was developed over a festival shopping center with specialty retail and boutique shops and fine restaurants. Separating the retail area on the ground floor and the office building above is a three-story parking garage. The improvements were developed on a one-acre parcel in the mid-1980s and are in excellent condition. The client is a local banker seeking an appraisal.

There is a twist to this assignment which makes it a little more difficult than most. Two sets of interests are present in the property. The ground-floor festival shopping center, three-story parking garage, and underlying land are owned by a retail developer from Philadelphia, while the office building is owned by another party who acquired the air rights from the retail developer when the project was initiated. These air rights, which were acquired for $500,000, extend above the festival shopping and parking garage improvements from a height of 40 feet to 140 feet along a vertical corridor of 10,000 square feet (100 feet by 100 feet). Thus, the air rights are associated with 1,000,000 cubic feet above the surface. The deed conveying these rights includes a restriction stating that the air rights can be developed with up to 100,000 gross square feet of office space. No other uses are permitted. Included with the transfer of the air rights was the use of a specified number of parking spaces in the garage.

The client reports that her bank committed a construction/permanent loan to the office developer in 1986. After suffering five years of poor performance due to a downturn in CBD office market conditions and a national recession, however, the developer defaulted on the loan in 1991 and granted the office building and air rights to the bank in lieu of foreclosure. Since then the market and the performance of the office building have improved. Now the bank is seeking an appraisal for federal reporting and disposition purposes. The bank does not have a mortgage or ownership interest in the festival retail center, parking garage, or underlying surface land area, all of which remain in the sole ownership of the Philadelphia-based retail developer.

Solution

In this example the buyer paid the seller for the right to construct up to 100,000 square feet of office space in the air rights extending from 40 to 140 feet above the underlying surface, the festival shopping center, and the parking garage. This exchange is illustrated in Figure 9.4.

Figure 9.4 Transfer of Air Rights

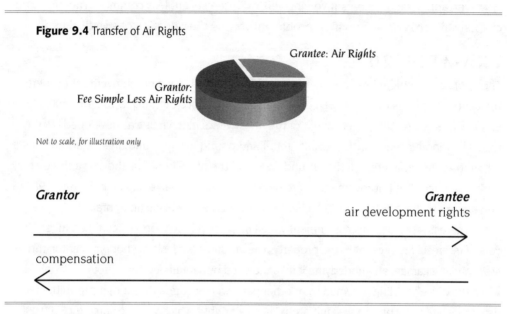

Grantee: Air Rights

Grantor:
Fee Simple Less Air Rights

Not to scale, for illustration only

Grantor   **Grantee**
                                        air development rights

compensation

The sales comparison approach is a good method to apply in such situations, but there are rarely sufficient sales data on comparable air rights in an area to make such an analysis possible. Unfortunately, transfers of air rights are scarce in all but a few highly developed urban areas, and the rights involved vary widely in detail and scope. Therefore, sole reliance on the sales comparison approach may not be possible and a rule-of-thumb approach is not accurate. In such cases, the combined application of the land extraction method of sales comparison and income approach techniques can be used to solve the appraisal problem. The land extraction method is demonstrated in this example, while income approach techniques are applied in Example 21.

The subject property is a 100,000-sq.-ft., Class A office building which lacks an ownership interest in the underlying land, garage, or retail center, but has easement rights in these properties for access and parking. To solve the valuation problem, the appraiser identifies and researches recent sales of comparable-quality office buildings in the CBD or surrounding areas. Next, the land value associated with these sales is deducted to yield the price allocated to the improvements. This improvement allocation becomes a unit of comparison. Then, sales of land comparable to the overall site, of which the air rights are part, are researched and analyzed to estimate the value of the underlying site as if whole. The percentage of value attributable to the air rights is then allocated from the overall site value. This percentage must be less than 100% and is generally less than 50%.

Assume the following data on improved property sales have been identified and researched:

Sale	Date	Location	Class	Price	Area in Sq. Ft.	Price/ Sq. Ft.
1	04/96	CBD	A	$11,250,000	75,000	$150.00
2	08/96	CBD	B	$15,000,000	150,000	$100.00
3	12/96	CBD	A	$15,625,000	125,000	$125.00

Further assume that all three sales enjoy waterfront locations in the CBD and waterfront land values are approximately $50.00 per square foot. Extracting land value from the sales yields the following improvement allocation:

Sale	Price	Land Area in Sq. Ft.	Land Value	Building Value	Building Value/Sq. Ft.
1	$11,250,000	40,000	$2,000,000	$ 9,250,000	$123.33
2	$15,000,000	35,000	$1,750,000	$13,250,000	$ 88.33
3	$15,625,000	42,000	$2,100,000	$13,525,000	$108.20

As the table shows, the two Class A office buildings (Sales 1 and 3) were sold at unit prices ranging from approximately $108 to $123 per square foot net of land, while the Class B office building (Sale 2) was sold at a unit price of $88.33 per square foot net of land. Since the subject property is a Class A office building and enjoys more convenient access to shopping and restaurants than the sale properties, a concluded value toward the high end of the range appears reasonable. Thus, a unit value of $125 per square foot may be estimated to yield the following value conclusion for the office building developed within the air rights:

100,000 square feet x $125 per square foot = $12,500,000

The next step is to estimate the value contribution of the air rights. As previously mentioned, downtown waterfront land sales indicate an overall site value of $50.00 per square foot. Applying this unit value to the subject's overall site area of 43,560 square feet yields a site value of $2,178,000. Now comes the tricky part—estimating the value contribution of the air rights. When sales of air rights in the area are not available, the appraiser must apply reasoned judgment. A site consists of three components—subsurface,

surface, and air rights—and the subsurface position has priority over the surface position, while the surface position has priority over air rights. In other words, the position of power decreases along a vertical scale.

The subject air rights consist of a vertical corridor 100 feet square from 40 feet to 140 feet, which is only a small portion of the total rights associated with the subject site. Therefore, only a small portion of the overall land value should be attributed to the air rights. In this example, the allocation is estimated at 20% to 25% of land value, arrived at through reasoned judgment. Thus, the value of the air rights alone is estimated to range from $435,600 ($2,178,000 x 0.20) to $544,500 ($2,178,000 x 0.25). Note, the air rights sold for $500,000 in the late 1980s, and market conditions have only recently begun to improve. Consequently, a value of $525,000 is concluded.

In summary, the value of the office building and associated air rights is estimated as follows:

Office building	$12,500,000
Air rights	$525,000
Total value	$13,025,000

EXAMPLE 21

The income approach can also be applied to solve this problem. In this application, the rental rates of comparable office space in the area are researched and compared to the subject, and any contract rent associated with leases is analyzed. From this rent analysis, the gross potential income of the property is forecast. Next, an allowance for vacancy and collection loss is deducted and the absorption of excess vacancy is projected. Finally, anticipated operating expenses, leasing costs, and tenant improvements are deducted to yield net operating income. This net income is capitalized into an indication of value if the property is operating at stabilized occupancy. If the property is not operating at market levels, a discounted cash flow analysis is performed to reflect the costs associated with bringing the property up to stabilized occupancy. Finally, the value of the air rights is added to yield the final value of the property as improved.

Assume the average rental rate in the subject office building is $22.00 per square foot on a full service basis, with operating expenses forecast at $6.00 per square foot. Market research reveals the following rent and expense comparables:

Sale	Location	Class	Area in Sq. Ft.	Avg. Rent /Sq. Ft.	Basis	Operating Exp./Sq. Ft.
1	River CBD	A	75,000	$22.00	Full service	$6.00
2	River CBD	B	150,000	$19.00	Full service	$5.50
3	River CBD	A	125,000	$21.50	Full service	$6.25

The subject rental rate of $22.00 per square foot and operating expenses of $6.00 per square foot appear reasonable and in line with the market. Assuming the subject occupancy rate is currently 90%, mirroring that of competing riverfront office buildings, the net operating income can be estimated as follows:

Potential gross income

100,000 sq. ft. x $22.00/sq. ft.	$2,200,000
Less 10% allowance for vacancy and collection loss	$220,000
Effective gross income	$1,980,000

Less operating expenses:

100,000 sq. ft. x $6.00/sq. ft.	$600,000
Reserves @ $0.20/sq. ft.	20,000
Net operating income	$1,360,000
	$13.60 per sq. ft.

If market research reveals a building capitalization rate of 11%, the value of the building exclusive of underlying site area would be calculated as follows:

$$
\frac{\$1,360,000}{0.11} = \$12,363,636
$$

Adding the air rights value of $525,000 estimated in the preceding example yields a final value estimate of $12,888,636, which is rounded to $12,900,000.

Building value	$12,363,636
Air rights value	525,000
	$12,888,636

SUMMARY

Physical divisions of real property create horizontal and vertical interests. The most common horizontal divisions are those associated with the subdivision and assemblage of land. In the subdivision process, a large parcel is broken up into smaller parcels; assemblage involves gathering together smaller parcels to form a new, larger parcel. Both activities are undertaken only if the end result proves more valuable and profitable for the investor.

Vertical divisions are perpendicular to horizontal divisions and include surface, subsurface, and air rights. Theoretically, the real property rights associated with a parcel of real estate extend from the core of the earth upward to the outer limits of the atmosphere. Subsurface rights generally pertain to mineral, mining, or tunnel rights. The separation of subsurface or air rights from a property can have a significant impact on the value and use of the remaining estate.

CHAPTER TEN

EPILOGUE

This text has explored the appraisal of partial interests. It includes an overview of real property theory and examples involving various income, legal, and physical divisions of property such as leased fee, leasehold, sandwich lease, mortgage, life estate, conservation easement, transferable development right, fractional, and vertical and horizontal interests. To solve the problems posed in the examples, all three traditional approaches to value were applied—the cost, sales comparison, and income approaches. Selecting the proper approach depends on the problem at hand and the supply of market data available for analysis. Clearly, partial interests are numerous and a common subject of appraisal assignments.

The real estate marketplace is dynamic and new problems and opportunities seem to be emerging at an ever-increasing pace. In the near future, more exotic partial interest scenarios may become prevalent. Appraisers may be asked to value water rights; wetlands, air pollution, and chlorofluorocarbon (CFC) mitigation rights; and vested concurrency rights, to name a few. The solutions of the past may not be appropriate for the problems that emerge in the future.

In the wake of the Great Depression, the appraisal industry created a niche for itself by solving the market's problems with unbiased, third-party analysis. This service will always be needed in one form or another. By applying creative thinking, seasoned judgment, and adaptive valuation methodologies, the appraisal industry will remain vital into the 21st century.